Stock Trading Techniques
Based on Price Patterns

Techniques for discovering, analyzing and using price patterns in the short-term and day trading of the stock market.

Michael Harris

Traders Press, Inc.®
PO Box 6206
Greenville, SC 29606

Teresa Darty Alligood
Editor & Graphic Designer

1975~2000
25th Anniversary

Traders Press, Inc.®
PO Box 6206
Greenville, SC 29606

*Dedicated
to
Shane,
Corbin
and Wyatt*

TRADERS PRESS, INC.®
PO BOX 6206
Greenville, SC 29606

Publishers of:

A Complete Guide to Trading Profits (Paris)
A Professional Look at S&P Day Trading (Trivette)
Ask Mr. EasyLanguage (Tennis)
Beginner's Guide to Computer Assisted Trading (Alexander)
Channels and Cycles: A Tribute to J.M. Hurst (Millard)
Chart Reading for Professional Traders (Jenkins)
Comparison of Twelve Technical Trading Systems (Lukac, Brorsen, & Irwin)
Cyclic Analysis (J.M. Hurst)
Day Trading with Short Term Price Patterns (Crabel)
Exceptional Trading: The Mind Game (Roosevelt)
Fibonacci Ratios with Pattern Recognition (Pesavento)
Futures Spread Trading: The Complete Guide (Smith)
Geometry of Markets (Gilmore)
Geometry of Stock Market Profits (Jenkins)
Harmonic Vibrations (Pesavento)
How to Trade in Stocks (Livermore)
Hurst Cycles Course (J.M. Hurst)
Investing by the Stars (Weingarten)
Jesse Livermore: Speculator King (Sarnoff)
Magic of Moving Averages (Lowry)
Market Rap: The Odyssey of a Still-Struggling Commodity Trader (Collins)
Pit Trading: Do You Have the Right Stuff? (Hoffman & Baccetti)
Planetary Harmonics of Speculative Markets (Pesavento)
Point & Figure Charting (Aby)
Point & Figure Charting: Commodity and Stock Trading Techniques (Zieg)
Profitable Grain Trading (Ainsworth)
Profitable Patterns for Stock Trading (Pesavento)
Short-Term Trading with Price Patterns (Harris)
Stock Market Trading Systems (Appel & Hitschler)
Stock Patterns for Day Trading (Rudd)
Stock Patterns for Day Trading 2 (Rudd)
Study Helps in Point & Figure Techniques (Wheelan)
Technically Speaking (Wilkinson)
Technical Trading Systems for Commodities and Stocks (Patel)
The Amazing Life of Jesse Livermore: World's Greatest Stock Trader (Smitten)
The Opening Price Principle: The Best Kept Secret on Wall Street (Pesavento & MacKay)
The Professional Commodity Trader (Kroll)
The Taylor Trading Technique (Taylor)
The Traders (Kleinfeld)
The Trading Rule That Can Make You Rich* (Dobson)
Trading Secrets of the Inner Circle (Goodwin)
Trading S&P Futures and Options (Lloyd)
Understanding Bollinger Bands (Dobson)
Understanding Fibonacci Numbers (Dobson)
Viewpoints of a Commodity Trader (Longstreet)
Wall Street Ventures & Adventures Through Forty Years (Wyckoff)
Winning Market Systems (Appel)

PLEASE CONTACT **TRADERS PRESS** TO RECEIVE OUR CURRENT 100 PAGE CATALOG DESCRIBING
THESE AND MANY OTHER BOOKS AND GIFTS OF INTEREST TO INVESTORS AND TRADERS.
800-927-8222 ~ Fax 864-298-0221 ~ 864-298-0222 ~catalog@TradersPress.com

Table of Contents

SECTION ONE
Setting the Foundation

SECTION FOUR
Pattern Library

Preface

Investing in stocks has entered a whole new domain in the late 1990's. The emergence of online brokerages coupled with the abundance of fundamental and technical information on every available stock issue has compelled hundreds of thousands of individuals from around the globe to seek their fortunes in the gold mines of the global stock markets. Going into this new millennium, the number of stock market investors and traders will increase dramatically as new tools become available that make it easier to access and process market information. Many have already quit their jobs and become full time traders, spending long hours in front of their personal computer screen and trying to profit from the volatile moves of stock prices. But, as easy as this may sound to the novice, making money trading stocks, or anything with a price tag on it for that purpose, is a very difficult task that requires more than the will or the wish to succeed!

Writing a book on a subject like this is a very challenging task, as there is plenty of good literature available by many distinguished authors. I intend to take upon this challenge, however, and provide the reader with new and valuable information, a result of my many years of research and development effort in this area.

Michael Harris

Acknowledgments

The author wishes to thank *Ed Dobson* and *Teresa Darty Alligood* at **Traders Press, Inc.®** for their professional publishing services.

The author wishes to express his gratitude to **Omega Research, Inc.**, and especially to *Mrs. Janette Perez* and *Mr. Kevin Feuerlicht*, for their offer of a complimentary copy of TradeStation 2000i, which was used to create the charts in this book.

Abbreviations

APS	Automatic Pattern Search
CPF	Combinatorial Pattern Formation
EPS	Exhaustive Pattern Search
DPI	Daily Pattern Identification
PCM	Pattern Combination Models
NDP	Next Day Projection
BSG	Bar Sequence Grouping
PLG	Profit and Loss Grouping
CRTS	Constant Risk Trading System
VRTS	Variable Risk Trading System

LIST OF FIGURES

LIST OF TABLES

Introduction

Trading stocks using price patterns has attracted a lot of attention in the last few years, mainly due to the dramatic increase in day and short-term position traders. Stock price action is now easily and cheaply available and can be monitored by the trader using the latest technological tools. This facilitates the easy incorporation of price patterns in the trading decision process.

There are many publications that deal with the subject of patterns. In most cases the context is limited to specific pattern formations and how they can be applied to day or position trading.

The material in this book focuses on three main objectives; first, to provide a basic theoretical framework dealing with the subject of patterns; second, to illustrate ways of discovering price patterns using historical stock data; and third, to demonstrate how patterns can fit in a systematic trading methodology.

The book is divided into four sections. Section one is entitled "Setting the Foundation" and contains chapters 1 through 4. Specifically, chapter 1 is a general discussion on the subjects of trading and price patterns, chapter 2 provides some basic definitions and framework and chapter 3 gives a classification of the different patterns types. Chapter 4 discusses how patterns are analyzed and used in actual stock trading, including setting up the trading rules and the entry/exit points. Special emphasis is given to the performance analysis of patterns with the use of specific examples.

Section Two is entitled "Discovering Stock Patterns," contains chapters 5 through 7 and deals with the subject of finding price patterns from historical stock data. In chapter 5, I outline a procedure for price pattern searching based on a trial-and-error, visual inspection method. Chapter 6, Discusses two methods for automating the search for historical price patterns. Chapter 7 presents a method to identify patterns as the market is form ing them. Also included is the p-Indicator, a new technical indicator based on patterns and the first of its kind.

Section three is entitled "Trading Methods and Systems Based on Price Patterns" and contains chapters 8 through 12. Chapter 8 describes manual trading techniques that do not require the use of a computer. Chapter 9 and chapter 10 deal with the subjects of system modeling and back-testing. Chapter 11 Shows how patterns may be grouped together to form a mechanical trading system. Chapter 12 is a discussion on how to use pattern based trading systems effectively, including some advanced capabilities of such systems and chapter 13 offers a basic discussion on money management.

Section Four is a library of specific price patterns, for several stocks, that have been found using the automatic pattern search methods I have developed. For each pattern listed, I describe its characteristics, the graphical chart formation, programming logic and EasyLanguage code, so it can be readily used in a trading system model. I then list the back-testing results for several stocks.

The reader may notice the absence of unnecessary references to stock charts this is often the case with many publications in this subject. The objective of this book is not to overwhelm the reader with charts and past entry and exit points of hypothetical trading system back-testing results but to provide a methodology and framework that can be of real value when developing a trading system.

This book is the result of a lifetime of research and development in the field of price patterns and trading system development. The algorithms and software used to discover the short-term price patterns that are listed in section four have taken many years to develop and substantial resources have been invested along the way. I certainly hope that the reader will benefit from the material presented and use it as a foundation for further development. At many instances, throughout the book, the reader may think that the concepts presented are painstaking and elaborate. Keep in mind, however, that trading stocks profitably is not an easy thing to accomplish and there are no simple ways or methods that do not require time and effort spent on the part of the trader, as well as any assumption of monetary risk. Trading is a long journey and being successful in it requires a combination of hard work and continuing effort. Let us keep this last comment in mind while turning the page to Section One.

SECTION ONE

SETTING THE FOUNDATION

THE NEED FOR A FRAMEWORK

Price patterns are becoming very popular as stock and commodity futures traders are discovering their advantages over conventional market timing techniques. Trading systems based on patterns are designed to take advantage of intraday or short-term price action and generate profits. While there are many publications describing specific patterns and their application to trading stocks and futures, there is a definite lack of a basic framework that addresses the subject.

The need for a framework arises not only from academic considerations but also from a practical perspective. Many traders tend to overlook the need for understanding the philosophy behind a trading methodology or technique but seem to only be interested in the immediate gratification that making a profit brings. Well, let me put it this way: *no one should expect to profit in the long-term from something that he or she does not understand to a reasonable extent*. The justification for this can be found in the stories of the large scores of traders that have lost a bundle trading. I have even known of traders that would use indicators and formulas like, for instance, RSI or moving averages, without even knowing how these things are calculated. There is no ground for anyone to believe that success will come in such a demanding and competitive arena like trading without having a basic knowledge of the underline principles and techniques.

In this section, I attempt to provide some insight on price patterns and how they can be used to trade stocks. This will also serve as a foundation for sections two and three, where methods to discover patterns are discussed and then combined together to form full-scale trading system models.

Chapter One

Background

Frequently Asked Questions

What is a Pattern?

A pattern is a bar chart formation that can be identified in the price history of a security. Usually, this type of chart formation has several past occurrences and is expected to re-occur in the future. Furthermore, whenever traders refer to a pattern, they often mean a "good" pattern, *i.e.* a chart formation that can be used to trade with a high probability of success.

How are Patterns Formed?

Although stock prices move mostly in random, they often cause the formation of distinct patterns. These patterns repeat in the future, as long as the same conditions that caused their origination repeat as well. Examples of conditions that may trigger the formation of patterns include technical analysis considerations, the release of Economic Indicators, stock upgrades or downgrades, earnings reports and insider buying or selling, these are just a few.

WHY USE PATTERNS?

A pattern is easy to identify, even under real-time conditions, all that is required for this is a basic charting software program. The daily or intraday stock price data needed is now easily accessible and available at low cost. Furthermore, patterns are formed by underline price action and a trader can solely base any buy or sell decisions on the pattern formation, ignoring any fundamental factors from the analysis. The reason for this is the very same existence of patterns assumes that all the fundamental information about a stock is already build in its price action. When this fails to be the case, and sometime does, an otherwise profitable pattern may result in a false trading signal and trading losses.

WHEN TO USE PATTERNS?

Patterns are suitable for day and short-term position trading of markets that have sufficient liquidity. Patterns do not (and cannot) predict long-term market direction. They are also not useful in illiquid or inefficient markets.

A FEW NOTES ON PATTERNS TRADING

GENERIC PATTERNS DO NOT EXIST

Many authors and investment conference speakers attempt to impress the reader by claiming that they have identified patterns that can be used to trade everything, a sort of generic trading method. While they show some historical performance results for a few stocks over a specific time period, they omit showing other examples of stocks or time periods where the particular patterns fail to generate acceptable results, or even generate unacceptable losses.

The mere fact is that patterns tend to be specific to a particular stock. However, one may find a specific pattern formation that will work for a group of stocks. The explanation for this may be partly found in the fact that stocks in a certain market sector tend to move in tandem while they have a negative correlation with stocks in other market sectors. To get to the bottom of this is probably the subject of extensive academic research. What is important for the reader to know is that one must be very careful in applying patterns found for one stock to other stocks before a detailed historical performance study is carried out. Some patterns may work for other stocks but others may not work at all.

MANY PATTERNS ARE REQUIRED TO TRADE PROFITABLY

Another fact that is often omitted from discussions on the subject is that in order to be profitable in the long term, either as a day trader or short-term trader, one must use a large number of patterns and trade several non-correlated markets. The latter is required in order to diversify market risk. The large number of patterns is needed to increase the number of market entry and exit signals, and thus increase the statistical significance of the trading process. What are the minimum requirements in terms of the number of patterns and markets traded is again a question that may be best answered by academic research.

As a practical guideline, one that is based solely on my own experience, at least two low correlation markets must be traded and three to four trading signals per month generated, in the case of short-term trading. In the case of day trading, at least one signal per day per market traded must be generated. As the frequency of trading signals increases, so are the chances of making a long term and consistent profit.

MATHEMATICAL DESCRIPTIONS ARE NECESSARY

This is not good news for those who avoid math! However, day and short-term trading require firm market entry and exit points. This dictates that the logic of the patterns is available in some quantifiable form. Fuzzy pattern forms cannot be used effectively since the corresponding performance cannot be known before hand. Here, I must make a distinction between traditional chart patterns and price patterns applicable to day and short-term trading. Traditional chart patterns, like double bottoms, wedges and triangles, are fuzzy geometric formations that can be identified by looking at bar charts. Unless one can describe them in a usable mathematical form and study their historical performance characteristics, it is not recommended that they be considered in actual trading. In contrast, the patterns described in this book, often called price patterns, are bar chart formations that can be described in exact mathematical form. In other words, traditional chart patterns pose a probability in both their formation and in making a profit. Price patterns have a probability in making a profit but are exact in formation. This is a huge difference and one that can result in widely different trading approaches. If one is unable to describe a pattern in a mathematical form and study its historical performance results, I do not recommend using it in actual trading.

GETTING THE PATTERNS IS HALF THE JOB

Becoming a profitable trader and staying one for a long period of time requires more than just a hand-full of patterns. It also requires a trading methodology that is compatible with the psycho-synthesis of the individual trading. Both elements in synergy, the trading system and the methodology, comprise a systematic trading approach. Trading using patterns can be a very demanding task that requires constant monitoring of the markets and continuing research. A trader must stay focused on the objectives and avoid actions that are outside of the scope of the trading method(s) used. Experience has shown that this may be as difficult as finding profitable patterns or systems in general. It is a matter of a discipline that must be developed over time and under actual trading conditions with real money at risk.

A FEW REMARKS ON TRADING TIME FRAMES AND TECHNIQUES

There are three main time frames used when trading the markets: day trading, short-term trading and long-term trading. Although a combination of any of these may be used, individual traders often adopt a trading style that fits into a specific trading time frame. This may be due to the fact that each different trading style requires different methodology, trading systems and effort put forth from the trader.

The two basic methods used in market forecasting are fundamental and technical. Both try to predict future price direction but with some distinct differences: *Fundamental methods* rely on economic data analysis along with the consideration of other factors such as political events, investment psychology and media involvement, to name a few. *Technical methods* rely on the analysis of price charts with the use of mathematics and geometry.

The use of technical methods has gained popularity in the last decade. This was also facilitated by advent of the personal computer, which allows implementation of these methods even under real-time conditions. Moreover, technical methods are well suited to the development of trading system models that implement "mechanical trading" and also allow the historical testing of trading performance. It is a widespread belief that mechanical trading via the use of a back-tested trading system model has more chances in the markets than a fundamental approach. As a consequence, technical methods have been in the epicenter of trader's attention for a while. On the other hand, there are those who insist that chart analysis and technical methods provide no information about the future and the results derived are of no real use.

Regardless of one's preference as to the basic method for predicting future market direction, some facts must be clearly understood: successful application of fundamental methods requires an in-depth knowledge of how the economic, social and political factors affect markets and all the associated information gathering which can be time consuming and expensive. Very few individuals can do this on their own, so this is left to Financial Institutions with a research department and a big budget to spend. Furthermore, fundamental methods are of little or no practical use to day and short-term traders since the time frames that they deal with do not allow the luxury of the necessary analysis and research. However, it is of paramount importance to long-term investors and even some government agencies that are mainly interested in future economic conditions.

Technical analysis comes to alleviate the need for understanding all the factors in fundamental analysis by assuming that all the information about a security is built in its underline price action. Therefore, all that is needed for a short-term prediction is careful analysis of past prices. However, any prediction made is valid only until the underline factors change and as a result, technical analysis is less applicable to predicting longer-term trends. It can be used with more success in day and short-term trading.

Day Trading

In day trading, trades can last from a few seconds to several hours. Usually, a day trader establishes a "flat" position by the market close and very rarely carries open positions overnight. In principle, a day trader tries to take advantage of small intraday price moves and profit. There are a whole variety of day trader types depending on the techniques used to achieve their goals. Most of the small players try to forecast intraday price direction using charting techniques and analysis that is provided by software programs that are available to them. Some big players attempt to assume the role of a market maker or specialist and profit from the difference in bid-ask spreads. In any case, the number of individuals who are pursuing day trading is increasing dramatically. This is further facilitated by the advent of Internet based online brokerage systems that offer flat rate executions along with a multitude of technical analysis tools and fundamental research. All this hype makes day trading look like an easy thing to do: just buy a computer and software, subscribe to an ISP, open an online trading account and there you go! You are a few clicks away from becoming independently wealthy! But wait, it is not as easy as it sounds…

The important question is whether it is possible for a trader to make money day trading. The answer is yes, but only if that trader does not belong to the 95% of those day traders that eventually lose money! The truth is, most day traders are destined to lose money because they do not understand how markets and the techniques they are using really work. On the other hand, even if a day trader is profitable, it is very difficult to accumulate substantial wealth. There is a multitude of inter-related factors that affect a day trader's performance over the long-term. Some are of psychological nature, such as lack of determination, fear and lack of discipline. Others are of technical nature, such as the ineffectiveness of most trading methods to predict intraday price changes, the lack of availability of timely data and the competition that comes from the market floor. A very common situation is when a day trader makes a long streak of small wins and then loses all profits made with just one bad trade. In some cases this can affect the trader's psychology to the extent of subsequent irrational trading behavior. This can widen losses and have severe consequences in one's professional and personal life.

Some have compared day trading to gambling. They have gone further to compare the act of looking at a computer quote screen and trading stocks to that of a casino slot machine. Some have even called Online Brokerages "Online Casinos!" While there may be some truth to this, depending on one's viewpoint, these characterizations are only appropriate to those who treat day trading as a gambling activity. They are addicted to pulling the trigger and actually do not care so much whether they are going to lose money or not. All of this, however, benefits the broker-age sector that makes huge profits from the fees charged to pro-vide day traders with real-time and cheap access to the markets. It also benefits those traders that do their homework and deal with the markets in a systematic way. They are usually the ones that pocket the trading losses of the gamblers!

Another factor that is of great importance to day trading suc-cess is commission size. Yearly commissions paid can amount to a significant percentage of the trading capital. In some cases, a day trader ends up putting all the effort and assuming all the risk, just to find out that the broker pocketed a significant por-tion of the profit made. This can easily happen, especially to a small size day trader, since the profits that can be made during the trading day are limited. Higher profit requires more trades that in turn causes commissions paid to accumulate.

Finally, day trading is a full time job and must be treated as such. Those that treat it as a recreational activity sooner or later realize that it is a very expensive one. Successful day trading requires constant monitoring of market prices and continuous research. This is probably the hardest aspect of it...

One must also try neglecting the assertions of the scores of authors and conference speakers who try to convince them of some easy and risk free way of making profits by day trading stocks. There is no such thing! They are just trying to generate hype and attract big audiences of people that think they can make easy money. The fact is that day trading is a very demanding activity that requires hard effort and deep knowledge of the trading process and associated tools.

SHORT-TERM TRADING

A short-term trader tries to forecast short-term price direction and take a position that will result in a trading profit. This type of trading is also called "position trading" or "swing trading." Regardless of what it is called, trades may last from one to several days, depending on the particular market traded and profit objectives.

In order to profit from short-term price moves, a market-timing model must be available and implemented. Placing a position a day in advance or a day later can result in a trading loss. This presents a real and very difficult problem since, in the short-term, markets move mostly in a random fashion. The objective of a short-term trader is to determine those exact times that there is a high probability that prices will move in a specific direction, irrespectively of the longer term trend. This can only be done effectively in a systematic manner and that creates the need of a timing model that filters out market noise while possessing appropriate performance characteristics.

Traditional technical analysis formulas such as Moving Averages and Indicators such as Relative Strength Index and Directional Moving Index, among many, are not very effective as short-term trading tools. Their signals have a time lag in following short-term moves and thus are unable to make a timely forecast. A more effective method of trading short-term is with the use of *Historical Price Patterns*. Traditional chart patterns, like heads & shoulders, double bottoms and triangles, can be theoretically used in short-term trading but in practice identifying them is a difficult task and often by the time a confirmation takes place it is too late to take the trade.

The size of commissions paid is rarely an issue affecting performance in short-term trading since the profits are usually much higher in proportion. Furthermore, there are short-term trading methods that do not require constant monitoring of market prices. This is a relief, as compared to the requirements of day trading, but there is a catch: In order to be successful as a short-term trader, one must have a trading system that predicts short-term price direction. There is a skepticism whether trading systems exist or can be developed that profit from short-term price moves for an extended period in time. Although the marketplace is filled with ads of "holy grails" that can make fortunes in a month's time, most of these systems do not perform under real trading conditions. Developing a trading system that can make profits consistently by trading short-term is a very challenging task that may take several years to accomplish.

Longer Term Trading

Markets do not always move sideways but often form long and protracted price trends. The objective of a longer-term trader is to "ride" those long trends and stay invested in the market for as long as a profit can be made. This is also called "trend trading" or "trend following." The trend duration may be months or even years in extreme cases, depending on one's measure of what constitutes a trend. The interpretation of what a trend is can be very subjective. For instance, let us consider the weekly chart of the Dow Industrials shown in figure 1-1. In hindsight, one may claim that there is a trend present that started early 1997. However, as shown in figure 1-2, another claim can be made that there is a trend since late 1994, which is still intact. The conclusion then is that what constitutes a trend is very subjective, depends on what one considers as the relevant investment horizon, and the actual trend size can only be known in hindsight.

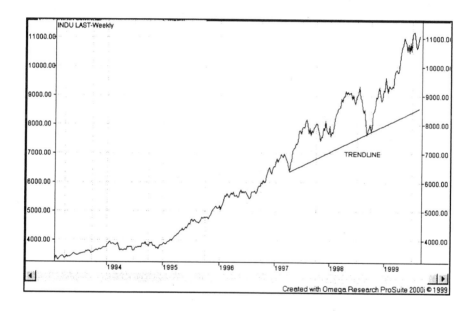

FIGURE 1-1: WEEKLY CHART OF DOW INDUSTRIALS - SHORT TREND

Longer-term traders use various fundamental and technical tools in order to determine possible points for trend initiation and termination. Capturing a trend in prices and successfully riding it is probably the dream of every serious trader or investor. However, it is, by far, one of the most difficult goals to accomplish in real life. There are many reasons for this difficulty, including market trend forecasting limitations and discipline from the part of the trader. Most traders rush to pocket short-term gains and that is a practice not well suited to longer trend trading.

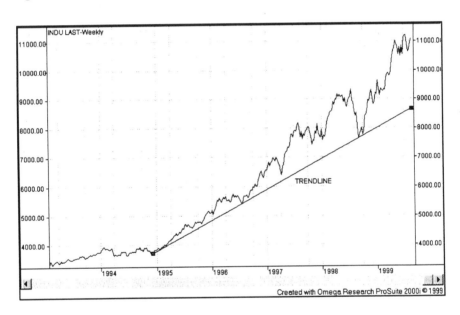

FIGURE 1-2: WEEKLY CHART OF DOW INDUSTRIALS - LONG TREND

Longer term trading has the highest profit potential because the trader can slowly accumulate positions along the direction of the trend. This can be done in spare time since it does not require following the market in real-time. So why is it that most people prefer to day trade for pocket change as compared to the profits that can be made from longer term trading? Part of the answer to this is possibly hidden in the desire of individuals to be a part of the daily trading game and part may be due to the fact that most people have consiously elected to have a shorter term view of life. After all, would it be possible for the markets to exist efficiently without the presence of day traders? An interesting question seeking for an answer!

Short-term trading systems based on price patterns can, under certain conditions, mimic the behavior of trend following systems. A relevant discussion is given in section three of this book.

Chapter Two

Definitions

A *pattern* is a bar chart formation that is made up of a number of consecutive price bars.

The *length* of the pattern, *l,* is defined as the number of price bars forming the pattern. A length equal to three, for instance, means that three consecutive bars form a pattern.

A chart *bar, b,* is defined as a vertical line that has a length equal to the price range during a specific time interval. If the time interval, for instance, is the whole trading day, then the length of the bar equals the daily trading range. In that case, it is called a *daily bar* and the chart a *daily bar chart.* If the time interval is any fixed number of minutes, five for instance, then we call that an *intraday bar* and the corresponding chart an *intraday bar chart.* Charts may be constructed using bars of any time interval ranging from a second to a month.

The upper end of a bar line is called the high, often denoted as H, and its lower end the low, often denoted as L. The open, O, of a bar is indicated by a horizontal tick extending left and the close, C, a horizontal tick, extending to the right of the bar, as shown in figure 2-1.

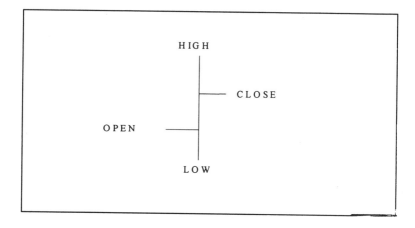

FIGURE 2-1: A CHART BAR

There are several visual variations of the chart bar shown in figure 2-1. These variations, (see figure 2-2), result from the relative position of the four parameters that define the price bar, the open, high, low and close. Some are more common and others are rarely found on a chart. The significance of these variations, as it relates to identifying patterns, will be discussed in section two.

A *bar sequence* of length, l, is defined as follows:

$$S = \{ b_0, b_1, \ldots, b_{l-1} \}$$

where the b_i's specify the quantities considered in each bar i. As an example, bar b_0 may be defined as follows:

$$b_0 = (H_0, L_0, C_0)$$

The above definition indicates that in the bar sequence only the high, low and close of bar 0 are considered. The open of the bar is not considered and its relative location in respect to the other three quantities is not important to this particular bar sequence. All bars in a pattern formation are defined in a similar way.

In general:

$$b_i = (O_i, H_i, L_i, C_i), \quad i = 1, 2, ..., l-1$$

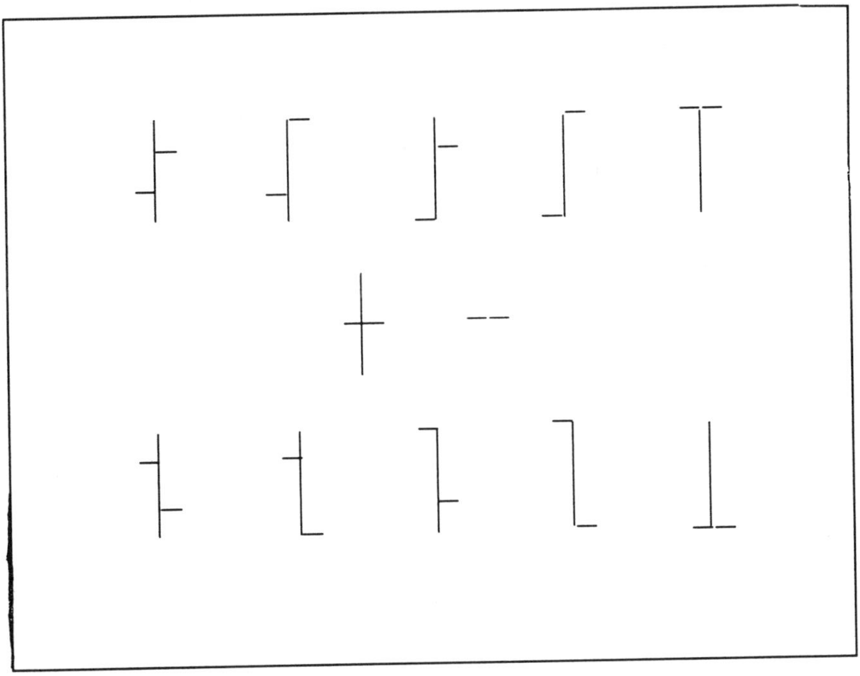

FIGURE 2-2: VARIATIONS OF A PRICE BAR

The numbering of the bars starts at 0 for the most recent bar, or first bar in the sequence, and increases thereafter. As an example, for a sequence length equal to three and daily bars, the number 0 denotes the last day, or today, 1 stands for yesterday and 2 for the day before yesterday.

Let us consider the following bar sequence:

$$S = \{ (C_0), (O_1,H_1,L_1,C_1), (H_2,L_2), (H_3,C_3) \}$$

According to the definitions given above, this sequence has a length of 4 bars. For the first bar, only the close is considered, for the second the open, high, low and close, for the third the high and the low, and for the forth the high and the close.

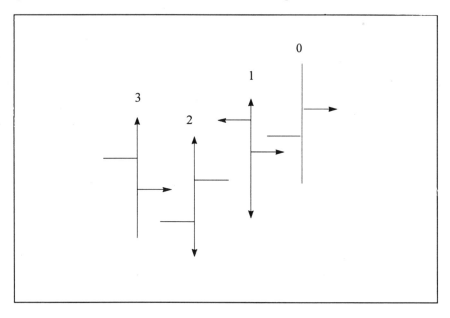

FIGURE 2-3: A BAR SEQUENCE GRAPHICAL EXAMPLE

We can present the above bar sequence in graphical form as shown in figure 2-3. The arrows found at selected locations on the bars indicate the quantities considered in it. Thus, the arrow on the close of bar 0 indicates that this is the only quantity considered in it, since no other arrow is present on that bar. On bar 1, all four parameters are labeled with arrows. On bar 2, only the high and the low have arrows on them, and finally, on bar 3 there are arrows on the high and the close.

The relative position and magnitudes of the parameters with arrows on them has been chosen arbitrarily in this example. The objective was only to show how to label the chart bars, which is important in the study of pattern formations. Next, a real pattern example is presented.

EXAMPLE: THE N-V PATTERN

Figure 2-4 shows a daily bar chart of Microsoft Corporation, (MSFT), for a time period between July and August 1999. Shown on the chart are two occurrences of a pattern, which is formed by four daily bars. These two separate occurrences are enclosed in rectangles for illustration purposes. This pattern was identified using a search method described in section two of this book. The bar sequence of the pattern has the following form:

$$S = \{(C_0), (C_1), (C_2), (C_3)\}$$

The bar sequence above indicates that only the close of each bar is considered in the pattern formation. Therefore, the relative location of the remaining parameters that define the bars that form the pattern is not of any importance. This is the reason that, although the two occurrences of the pattern on figure 2-4 may appear slightly different, they describe the same pattern when just the closes are considered. This is further shown in figure 2-5 where, for all practical purposes, all of the parameters of no importance have been set equal. Also shown is a graphic representation of the pattern obtained by joining together the bar closes with lines (line chart). Due to the shape of the graphic, I call this the N-V pattern (N-V).

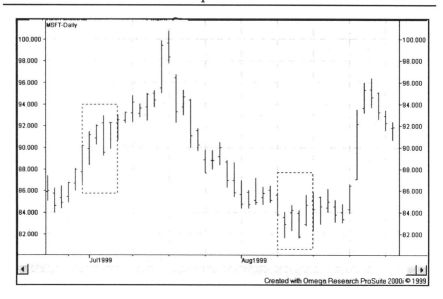

FIGURE 2-4: A BAR CHART AND PATTERN FOR MICROSOFT CORPORATION

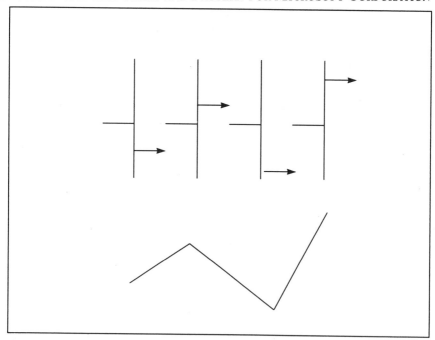

FIGURE 2-5: THE N-V PATTERN

The N-V pattern is found in daily chart data and can be used to take long positions in many stocks, including that of Microsoft. The trade is entered at the open of the day following the pattern formation. The pattern logic is very simple and it can be easily monitored either manually or with the help of charting software. One can even describe this simple pattern in English language form as follows:

If the close of today is higher than the close of 2 days ago and the close of 2 days ago is higher than the close of 3 days ago and the close of 3 days ago is higher than the close of yesterday then buy tomorrow on the open.

A profit target and a protective stop must be placed and are usually equal to a given percentage of the trade entry price.

Details on the parameters of the N-V pattern and its historical performance may be found in section four of this book.

Chapter Three

Pattern Types

This chapter presents several different pattern types that may be identified in historical stock data. The classification of patterns into different types is needed when searching stock data with the objective of finding price formations that meet certain performance criteria. Unless one knows what it is that he or she is looking for, it will be very hard to identify it!

Here I must make a distinction between the terms "pattern type" and "pattern logic." The word "type" refers to a general description of a pattern used in a classification mechanism. The word "logic" refers to the actual pattern structure that helps comparing patterns and studying their historical performance.

Patterns can only be compared in the sense of an algorithm. Two patterns that look similar using one specific algorithm, may seem quite different using a different algorithm. Patterns that have multiple occurrences, all looking visually alike, are just special cases in the vast universe of abstract mathematical pattern types.

Exact Patterns:

This type of pattern is the most commonly used and easily understood. I call it "exact" because every occurrence of the pattern in the history of a stock matches 100% all of the remaining occurrences, of course, in the sense of an algorithm. Furthermore, this type of pattern has multiple occurrences that are easy to compare visually. However, proportions are not kept to ratio, just the relative position of the bars in the chart formation are kept constant. Figure 3-1 shows an example of two occurrences of an exact pattern. The length of this pattern is equal to 4 bars. It may be seen that the relative position of all bars in each of the two occurrences is the same. However, bar 3 in the first occurrence is longer than the corresponding bar 3' of the second occurrence. Also, the relative position of the close of bar 0 with respect to the high is different than that of the corresponding bar 0'. Despite these two minor differences, the two pattern occurrences look alike to the naked eye.

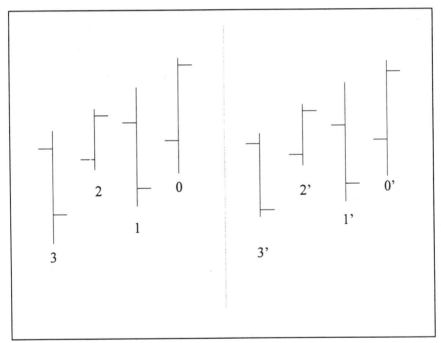

FIGURE 3-1: TWO OCCURRENCES OF AN EXACT PATTERN

MATCHED:

The occurrences of this pattern type match each other at a minimum desired "matching level," expressed as a percentage. The "matching" is true only in the sense of the algorithm used, i.e. it is a mathematical comparison and any two occurrences of a matched pattern may not visually look alike at all. The degree of matching can be selected arbitrarily but levels above 50% are usually needed to produce desirable results. A matching level of 100% results in an "exact" type pattern, by definition.

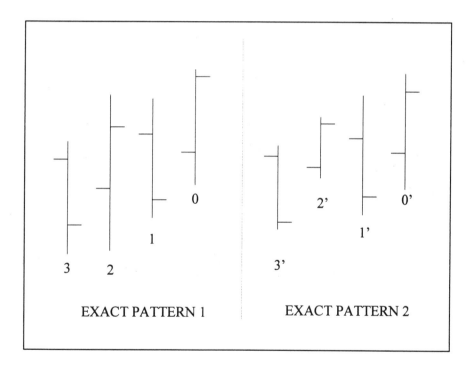

FIGURE 3-2: TWO OCCURRENCES OF A MATCHED PATTERN

27

Another way to look at matched patterns is as sets that are formed by the union of subsets of exact patterns. The patterns of each subset match the patterns of all other subsets at the desired matching level or higher. Each subset defines a distinct exact pattern with its own number of occurrences in the history of a stock. The limiting case is when each subset has only one occurrence that matches the remaining subsets at a 100% level, which is the definition of an exact pattern. In that case, the number of subsets also coincides with the number of occurrences of the exact pattern.

Figure 3-2 illustrates the concept of a matched pattern by showing two different exact patterns. Each of the exact patterns belongs to a subset and has a given number of historical occurrences. The union of the subsets forms the matched pattern set. A close inspection shows that the two patterns resemble a lot but are not quite the same. The degree of "resemblance" relates to the percent matching level.

PROPORTIONAL:

These are patterns with occurrences of same proportions, in terms of the daily ranges of the price bars, expressed as the distance between the highs and the lows. That is, the ratio of the first bar range to the second bar range is the same in all occurrences. The same holds for the ratio of the second bar to the third, the ratio of the third to the forth, and so on. The motivation in searching for this type of patterns is to discover some kind of geometric symmetry that is often hidden in seemingly random data.

DELAY:

Delay patterns can be patterns of any type where the order entry occurs with a delay. With a delay pattern, instead of entering a position at the close of the bar that the pattern is formed or at the open of the next bar, the position is entered after a certain number of bars, called the "delay." The delay period can be several bars long, depending on the pattern found by a search algorithm. The motivation in searching for this type of pattern comes from the fact that some, otherwise profitable, pattern formations indicating a position to be taken in a certain direction, suffer an immediate correction due to profit taking. The delay used allows filtering out the correction and taking a position when prices resume direction.

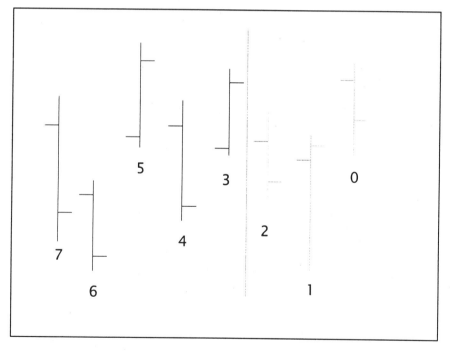

FIGURE 3-3: EXAMPLE OF A DELAY PATTERN

Figure 3-3 shows a pattern with a delay period equal to three, for illustration purpose only. The actual pattern is made up of the five bars labeled 3, 4, 5, 6 and 7. The remaining bars, 2, 1 and 0, are shown with dotted lines indicating that their relative position on the chart is not of any importance to the pattern formation, as well as the associated price action. Position initiation, whether that is a long or short, occurs at the open or close of bar 0. Note that the delay period is the same for all occurrences of the same pattern.

SPLIT:

These are patterns that are formed by a series of different but consecutive pattern types, a first and a second, in the simplest case. Every occurrence of the same Split pattern has identical corresponding parts, whether they are of the exact, matched, proportional or, in the case of the second pattern, a delay type. In addition, the two parts must be in the same order in the split pattern formation, for all the occurrences. When comparing split patterns, the algorithm used should match each of the two parts, or two patterns, separately.

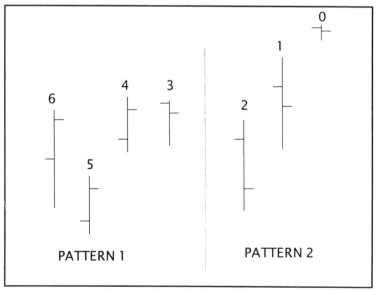

FIGURE 3-4: A SPLIT PATTERN

The motivation in searching for split patterns is twofold: First, split patterns have a greater number of bars in their formation. This happens since the splitting of a pattern into two parts greatly reduces the number of conditions that an algorithm must match and therefore increases the number of occurrences. Secondly, a split pattern may have a higher probability of success since the second pattern can be used as a confirmation to the first pattern indication for a position entry in a certain direction, long or short.

Figure 3-4 shows a split pattern made of two patterns. The first pattern is made up of 4 bars and the second of 3. Each pattern in the formation is considered separately and the relative position of the bars of the first pattern with respect to the second pattern is not relevance, as each part is considered separately.

When matched pattern types form a split pattern, each part must be matched to its own desired matching level. Usually, the last part of the split pattern is matched to a higher level than the first, as it is the final formation before taking a position.

OVERLAY:

Overlaying a number of patterns forms the pattern type. The simplest case is when there are only two different patterns. The only restriction is that the last bars of each of the patterns coincide. In the simple case, where the overlay pattern is formed by two patterns, the last bar of the first pattern must also be the last bar of the second pattern. Each pattern in the formation can have a different length and can be of different type. Every occurrence of the same overlay pattern must have identical corresponding patterns, whether they are of the exact, matched or proportional type. When comparing overlay patterns, an algorithm should match each of the parts, or patterns, separately.

The motivation in searching for Overlay patterns is to use the pattern with the shorter length as a confirmation to the trading signal given by the pattern with the longer length. In this way it may be possible to increase the probability of trading success.

In the case of an overlay pattern made up of matched pattern types, each part is matched to a minimum desired matching level. Usually, the shorter length pattern is matched to a higher level than the longer length pattern.

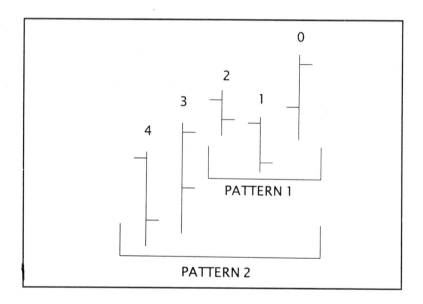

FIGURE 3-5: OVERLAYING PATTERNS

An example of an overlay type pattern is shown in figure 3-5. It is formed by two patterns. The first is made up of 3 bars and the second of 5 bars. Bars 0, 1 and 2 are common to both patterns.

INTER-MARKET:

These are patterns of any type that are discovered by searching the data of a stock, but indicate a position to be taken in another stock. For instance, a pattern can be found that when formed in a gold stock signals a position in a utility stock. This happens due to the apparent interdependence of some markets, as investors keep shifting assets from one to sector to the other depending on prevailing economic conditions.

MATHEMATICAL DESCRIPTION OF PATTERN TYPES:

Let S be a bar sequence and **P** a pattern. Then:

$$\mathbf{P} = A\{S\}$$

where A is mathematical operator. Let us consider the following choices for A:

E: Exact
M_k: Matched, k = the matching level in percent
PR_n: Proportional, n = proportionality ratio

We can use the above operators to describe pattern types. For instance, an exact pattern is defined as follows:

$\mathbf{P} = E\{S\}$

and a matched pattern as:

$\mathbf{P} = M_k\{S\}$, with matching level of k%

Please note that $M_{100}\{S\} = E\{S\}$, by definition.

A proportional pattern with 75% proportionality ratio is described as:

$$P = PR_{75}\{S\}$$

Next, consider the following composite operators:

S: Split
O: Overlay

A split pattern is defined as follows:

$P = S\{P_1, P_2\}$, and it is formed by linking the two patterns, one right after the other. The patterns, P_1 and P_2, can be of any type.

An Overlay pattern is defined as:

$P = O\{P_1, P_2\}$, and it is formed by two patterns, one overlaying the other but with the last bars of both coinciding. The two patterns can be of any type but can have different lengths.

Next, the Delay and Inter-Market operators are considered as:

D_j: Delay, $j = 1,2,3,\ldots,n$ the delay in bars
IM: Inter-Market

A delay pattern is defined as:

$P = D_j\{P_1\}$, P_1 being a pattern of any type.

An inter-market pattern is defined as:

$P = IM\{P_1\}$, an inter-market pattern of any type, P_1.

Below, the defined types and operators are used to describe several pattern formations:

$P = D_4\{E\{S\}\}$ is an exact pattern with 4 bars delay.

$P = D_7\{M_{95}\{S\}\}$ is a pattern matched at 95% level, that has 7 bars delay.

$P = S\{M_{75}\{S_1\},E\{S_2\}\}$ is a split pattern formed by linking two patterns, one matched at a 75% level and the other of the exact type.

$P = S\{M_{75}\{S_1\},M_{85}\{S_2\}\}$ is a split pattern formed by linking two matched patterns, one at 75% and the other at 85%.

$P = O\{E\{S_1\},M_{90}\{S_2\}\}$ is an overlay pattern formed by one exact pattern and a pattern matched at 90%.

$P = S\{M_{90}\{S_1\},D_3\{PR_{75}\{S_2\}\}\}$ is a split pattern formed by a pattern matched at 90% and a proportional pattern with 75% proportionality ratio and 3 bar delay in taking a position.

$P = IM\{S\{M_{65}\{S_1\},D_2\{E\{S_2\}\}\}\}$ is an inter-market - split pattern, formed by linking together a 65% matched pattern and an exact pattern with a 2 bars delay.

The pattern types presented in this chapter are useful in the design of an algorithm that searches historical data for price patterns. This task will be the subject of section two of this book. What was achieved in this chapter was to take the simple notion of a bar sequence S and create a vast number of possibilities for pattern formations. It is this very same process of creating these possibilities that gives value to the pattern based trading methodology. One simple reason for this is that out of the many alternatives one can search for, there is good probability that some will satisfy certain performance criteria. If that is the case, that may translate into trading profits. Being able to make a selection out of many choices is always better than struggling with only a few alternatives.

CHAPTER FOUR

PATTERN ANALYSIS

THE NEED FOR WELL DEFINED TRADING RULES

One of the most important aspects of a trading methodology is the establishment of a set of criteria and rules that facilitate its application apart from any ambiguity. This translates further into describing specifically how the methodology is to be applied under actual trading condition. Nothing can be worse than vague trading rules that provide no clue of when to initiate and close a position. This has always been the case with many "empirical" trading rules, as well as, with many well-known indicators and systems. As an example, I can mention the famous rule; "The trend is your friend." I hope that no one intends to base any trading actions on something as general and vague as this rule is, providing no useful information on when to establish a position or when to exit it. Of course, the trend is always a friend but could also be the cause of devastating losses if it is near its top or bottom! (How many times have you had a dear friend borrow money that he never returned?) Another vague rule that I can mention is "keep your profits run - cut your losses short." An excellent rule, but quite general and of no real use if not accompanied with specific guidelines of what an acceptable profit and loss is.

Unfortunately, the same holds true with many popular, almost all I would say, indicators and trading formulas in use. Although they provide signals to initiate positions, they fail to indicate when to exit them. The establishment of the exit point is left to trading system developer or trader. His or her task is to find another indicator or formula that will generate an exit signal. In my opinion, this is where most problems that emerge during the trading system development process start!

A complete set of short-term trading rules should contain the following:

1. Rules establishing the market entry point.

2. A profit target that defines the specific price level where the position must be exited with a profit.

3. A protective stop-loss that defines the specific price level the position must be exited at a loss.

4. The specific market(s) that the technique, system or pattern applies to.

5. The trading time frame(s) applicable, i.e. intraday, daily, weekly, etc.

Unless 1 through 5 above is well defined, then no one can claim the existence of a useful trading rule. This is also true in the case of patterns. They can be of real value if all the parameters that are required for their successful application are defined in advance. In fact, discovering profitable patterns involves an advanced definition of those parameters. This is contrary to some common views asserting that the process that generates the market entry signals can be separated from that of the exit signals. Although this is usually done as a matter of convenience in writing programming code, per se, it should not be confused as defining two separate processes that are of independent nature.

Because of the discussion above, all patterns that will be considered in this book are specific trading rules, in the context explained above. *Combining many of these trading rules with appropriate money management and operational methodology forms a complete trading system;* a concept explained in more detail in section three of this book.

DESCRIBING THE TRADING RULES

A trading rule defines the condition(s) that determines whether a pattern has been formed and a position needs to be placed. It is also called the pattern "logic." In general, trading rules can be as complicated as anyone may desire. In practice, it is widely accepted that the simpler trading rules have more chances in performing well.

Trading rules may be expressed as mathematical equations, logical propositions or a mixture thereof. Price patterns have the advantage that their logic consists of conditional statements that describe the relation of the parameters of the bars involved in their formation. Specifically, the parameters considered are the high, low, open and close of the each of the bars forming the pattern.

The following is an example of the structure of trading rules that define a simple pattern (for illustration purposes only):

If :   high of today > high of yesterday and
low of today > low of yesterday and
high of yesterday > low of today

Then: Enter a long position and Establish a profit target and protective stop price

The example above gives a general idea of the nature of the trading rules that describe patterns. One important feature of this type of trading rule is that it does not contain any variables that need adjusting, in their position entry part, as it is the case with traditional indicators and formulas. This prevents any variable optimization that can lead to a "fitted" system. Optimized or "fitted" systems are one of the main reasons for the failure of traditional technical trading methods that are based on indicators and formulas that include variables that can be varied by the user. It is a widespread practice to select the values for these variables by running a set of historical performance analysis results (back testing) while varying the parameter values and retaining those that give the "best" or optimum performance. It is now well understood that trading methods based on such practices have a very high probability of failure under actual trading conditions. As an example, I can mention the adjustment of the length of a moving average crossover until the best result or "fit" is obtained.

In contrast to the best "fit" practice, the patterns considered in this book do not contain any variables that can be varied and, consequently, optimized. I refer to these simple trading models as "pure," meaning that they are based solely on the comparison of price levels, as opposed for instance, to the mathematical averaging of prices taking place when using moving averages.

DEFINING THE ENTRY POINTS

The *entry point* is a specific price level where a newly generated trading signal indicates opening a position. The most commonly used entry points are:

- The close of a bar
- The open of a bar
- An intraday price level

The entry point used in conjunction with a specific pattern is not chosen arbitrarily but must be part of the pattern logic. Ignoring or altering the entry point may result in sizable deviations from expected performance.

THE CLOSE AS AN ENTRY POINT

The close of the last bar in a pattern bar sequence may be used as a position entry point. In the case of daily bars, the close of the last bar presents an important price level –often an indication of price direction and momentum. Furthermore, most traditional technical indicators are calculated using the close of daily bars. However, the close is not a very convenient entry point. This is especially true if the close of the last bar in a pattern's formation is also part of its logic or trading rules. In this case, it is possible that nearing the market close, prices are at such a level that one cannot resolve whether there is an entry point or not. Although this may not happen very often, whenever it does, it may create confusion, or even lead to a position entry that is not valid after closing price settlement. There are some ways of dealing with this issue including delaying the trade for the open of the next day or a pre-opening session, if any.

Another problem that one may face when using the close as an entry point is that of *signal tracking*. This refers to the process of establishing in real-time when a particular pattern formation is in effect and all trading rules that define it are valid. There are at least two ways of dealing with this problem: the *"next day projection" technique* (NDP) and that of *real-time monitoring* of the pattern logic and rules.

41

The "next day projection" technique requires that the pattern formation is monitored on a bar-by-bar basis to determine whether the next bar can turn it to a valid formation. The conditions that the next bar must satisfy are then extrapolated using the pattern known logic. Near the close, those conditions are evaluated to determine whether the pattern has a valid formation. If that is the case, then a position is placed at the close.

The real-time monitoring technique is a much more complicated method that requires a real-time market data feed and a software package that continuously evaluates the pattern logic as the data come through. In other words, as the market close nears, every tick must be treated as the market close. There are a few software packages that allow this type of operation in real-time, one is the TradeStation by Omega Research, Inc. The programming and successful operation of those packages requires special skills, knowledge and experience that only those with significant exposure to computers posses. For those that are not well versed with that kind of technology, the simpler method of projection will be discussed in more detailed in section three.

Despite the problems that often arise when using the close as an entry point, its importance should not be underestimated. Patterns that use the close often take advantage of "overnight" gaps in prices for a quick "hit" of the profit target. This results in a reduction of the average trade duration, which is very desirable in short-term trading.

THE OPEN AS AN ENTRY POINT

The open of the bar following the last bar in a pattern bar sequence is the most popular entry point. In the case of intraday data, the open of the next bar is the next tick after the close of the previous bar. In the case of daily bars, the open of the next bar often represents a whole new price level.

Most traders use the open because it is a convenient entry point. After the market close, a trading system may be re-evaluated to take into consideration the new price data and decide whether a trade needs to be placed by next day's open. That was especially true several years ago, when technical indicators needed to be evaluated either manually or using very slow computers. Today, even the most sophisticated and complex mathematical models can be evaluated in a matter of minutes or even seconds, using high-speed personal computers.

The use of the open price presents certain problems related to slippage, which is the difference between the open price and the actual price that an order if filled. This can result in deviations of the real trading performance as compared to the back-tested performance of a trading system. The slippage is much more pronounced when using the open as an entry point rather than the close. This also may happen because often the liquidity during the market open is usually much lower than the market close.

Despite any problems, the open represents a very important entry point and it is much more convenient than the close. After all, the only two points that can be defined on a price bar, as soon as they occur, are the open and the close. The rest, the high and low, can only be identified with certainty after the market close.

The advent of 24-hour trading poses certain problems with the use of the daily open or close as position entry points. However, it is very unlikely that 24-hour trading will ever become a full trading session, due to certain structural limitations in the global financial system, such as time differences and local trade clearance. It is also true that in times of high volumes and advancing stock markets the maintenance of 24-hour trading systems is economically justified, where in times of decreasing volume it becomes uneconomical. Nevertheless, such a possibility requires re-consideration of market entry points and it is currently a subject of interest and research.

INTRADAY PRICE LEVELS AS ENTRY POINTS

The use of intraday price levels is common both in day and short-term trading. An intraday price level may be defined as an already known high or low price of a previous bar, or even a specific price level. Often, if a long position is to be initiated, the intraday entry price level is above the market whilst it is below the market in the case of a short position. This serves two purposes: first to allow for a so called "confirmation" of the trading signal and second to guarantee that the trade will always be placed if the market moves in the appropriate direction.

The basic problem with intraday entries is that the liquidity of the market during the entry is not known in advance. This can present severe problems when the position stops are in the daily volatility range. In that case, market makers, floor brokers or specialists may "run" for the stop and then let prices resume direction. Therefore, it is important that intraday entry points are used only in very liquid markets, coupled with sizable stops. A small account day or short-term trader should never underestimate the fact that the big players know the game well and they have the ability to influence market direction for small, intraday moves. That is not market inefficiency but the way things are designed to work.

ESTABLISHING THE PROFIT TARGET AND STOP-LOSS

The profit target and stop-loss are an integral part of the pattern logic. They must also be included in any search process used to find patterns. Part of the explanation for this is that patterns are caused by price action caused by specific events, which, in turn, results in specific price re-action. Although the profit target and stop-loss may be varied to a certain extent, one should not expect that patterns exist that allow arbitrary selection of the profit target and stop-loss levels. Another way of explaining this is to realize that patterns are formed as a result of price volatility and the profit target and stop loss values are related to the magnitude of that volatility. (Incidentally, that is the reason that patterns are well suited to day and short-term trading. Their objective is to time short-term market moves rather than predict long term direction or market turning points.)

As an example, let us consider a pattern formed by three daily bars and another formed by seven daily bars. One should not expect the profit target and stop-loss levels for the three-day pattern to be of the same magnitude with that of the seven days. The reason for this is that the more history that the pattern carries in its formation the more ability it has to predict the future. Therefore, the three-day pattern often permits a smaller profit target and stop-loss than the seven-day pattern does.

PROFIT TARGETS

The *profit target* determines the price level to exit an open position, long or short, with a profit. In day and short-term trading the profit target exit price must be known in advance. There are two ways to express the profit target:

- As an increment
- As a percentage

When *increments* are used, they are often expressed in terms of points, ticks or actual dollars depending on the market traded.

Stock traders prefer to use dollar amounts whilst futures traders prefer ticks or points. Therefore, if a stock is bought at $55 1/8 and the profit target is $2 ½ then the profit target exit price is $55 5/8. In general:

For Long Positions:

Profit Target Exit Price = Entry price + Profit Target

For Short Positions:

Profit Target Exit Price = Entry price - Profit Target

Where:
Profit Target = A Dollar Amount Increment

Whenever *percentages* are used, they are expressed as real numbers, but always refer to the position entry price. As an example, if a stock is bought at $20 and the profit target is 5% then the profit target exit price is $21. In general:

For Long Positions:

Profit Target Exit Price = Entry price x (1 + Profit Target/100)

For Short Positions:

Profit Target Exit Price = Entry price x (1 - Profit Target/100)

Where:

Profit Target = G%, where G is a number greater than zero.

The use of the appropriate profit target is of great importance in the short-term trading of stocks using price patterns. While most people as accustomed to using price increments, percentages seem to be more appropriate for stocks. This fact has certain ramifications in the way historical performance is determined during back testing as well as how searching algorithms works and will be discussed in further detail in subsequent chapters. Here, the explanation for the preferred use of percentages is based on the fact that it allows maintaining uniformity in the time duration of the trades generated by a specific pattern along the price history of the stock. This is due to the fact that when the stock price is low the profit target is also low resulting in reasonable average trade duration. Likewise, when the stock price is high the profit target is proportionally higher and the time interval required hitting it is of similar average duration. In contrast, if a constant increment is used, then for periods of low stock price the time it takes to hit the profit target is much longer than during periods of high stock price. Essentially, a percentage profit target is equivalent to a variable increment size that is a function of the stock price, sort of a duration-adaptive target mechanism.

STOP-LOSSES

The *stop-loss* determines the price level to exit an open position, long or short, with a loss. In day and short-term trading the stop-loss exit price must be known in advance. There are two ways to express the stop-loss level:

- As an increment
- As a percentage

As with the case of a profit target, when *increments* are used, they are often expressed in terms of points, ticks or actual dollars depending on the market traded. Stock traders prefer to use dollar amounts while futures traders prefer ticks or points. Therefore, if a stock is bought at $55 1/8 and the stop-loss is $2

½ then the stop-loss exit price is $52 5/8. In general:
For Long Positions:

Stop-loss Exit Price = Entry price - Stop-loss

For Short Positions:

Stop-loss Exit Price = Entry price + Stop-loss

Where:
Stop-loss = Dollar Amount Increment

When *percentages* are used, they are expressed as real numbers, but always refer to the entry price. As an example, if a stock is bought at $20 and the stop-loss is 5% then the stop-loss exit price is $19. In general:

For Long Positions:

Stop-loss Exit Price = Entry price x (1 - Stop-loss/100)

For Short Positions:

Stop-loss Exit Price = Entry price x (1 + Stop-loss/100)

Where:

Stop-loss = S%, where S is a number greater than zero.

The use of the appropriate stop-loss is of great importance in the short-term trading of stocks using price patterns. While most people are accustomed to using price increments, percentages seem to be more appropriate in the case of stocks, for the same reasons explained in the case of profit targets. Furthermore, it is a common practice that the profit target and the stop-loss selected to be of the same type, whether increment or percentage.

PERFORMANCE ANALYSIS

A pattern should only be used in actual trading only after a detailed performance analysis is carried out for the market or markets that it applies to, or it is intended to be applied to. This can only be achieved correctly if all the parameters that define the pattern, as described earlier in this chapter, are available in advance.

The performance analysis is based on a historical study of the pattern performance. This is also called back testing. Accomplishing this task requires the availability of an appropriate length of historical data for the applicable market(s). The analysis can either be done manually or by the use of computer. A manual analysis is a very tedious process and it is not recommended unless one intends to use it as error checking to verify a few entries and corresponding exit points. This process can only be efficient with the use of a computer. For this purpose, one may write custom software code that reads in the historical data, checks to see if the trading rules are satisfied and then applies the appropriate profit target and stop-loss when an entry point is present.

Alternatively, one may use any of the available for these task software programs, which provide an integrated platform for trading system model back-testing and performance analysis. This is very convenient, since the programs "do all the work" for you. They allow describing trading rules in a high-level computer language, include historical databases and generate detail performance analysis reports. Since patterns have simple trading rules, even some popular charting software programs can be used to study historical performance.

In the case of a single pattern, the most important parameters considered in the performance analysis are shown on table 4-1.

PARAMETER	DESCRIPTION
N	Total number of trades generated
%P	Percentage of profitable trades
R_{WL}	Ratio of average winning to loss
C_L	Maximum consecutive losers
T_D	Average time in a trade
D_R	Maximum draw down

TABLE 4-1: COMMONLY USED PERFORMANCE PARAMETERS

The *total number of trades generated, N,* is a number equal to or smaller than the number of pattern *occurrences* in the stock price history. It can be smaller since one may elect to ignore an entry point while a position is in place, a not frequent but possible event. In general, the number of trades that a pattern generates should be high enough so that the remaining parameters carry some statistical significance. The minimum number of trades depends on the trading time frame used and has been a very controversial subject. Patterns for day trading that are analyzed over intraday data must generate a much higher number of trades than, for instance, patterns formed of daily bars. As a rule of thumb, I would avoid using any daily pattern that generates less than 20 trades over a sufficiently long history of data and any intraday pattern that generates less than a number equal to 20 times the number of the intraday bars, in the time frame considered. This empirical rule may be expressed as follows:

$$N > 20 * Nb$$

Where Nb the number of bars in the time frame considered, taking daily data as a basis and setting it equal to one. If the number of trades resulting from the performance analysis is less than the minimum number suggested above then the span of historical data must be increased up to the maximum history available for the specific stock. Unless a satisfactory number for the number of trades is obtained, it is not recommended to use the pattern in actual trading, as future performance may deviate significantly from the back-tested one.

Table 4-2 depicts the minimum number of trades that must be generated over a sufficiently long history of data for different trading time frames:

TIME FRAME	MINIMUM NUMBER OF TRADES
Daily	20
Hourly	130
Half - Hour	260
15 Minute	520
5 Minute	1560
1 Minute	7800

TABLE 4-2: MINIMUM NUMBER OF TRADES REQUIRED

Patterns based on weekly and monthly bars are not included in table 4-2 because they usually fail to generate sufficient samples. Those patterns may be better analyzed in the context of conventional chart analysis.

It is also evident from the table that as the bar time frame decreases the number of trades required increases fast. Then, no one should expect to find a pattern in, let us say, 5 minute data bars, test its performance, get a few trades, and expect that it will work well in the future. Incidentally, this is exactly what many "black-box" trading system developers do and omit to include it in their presentation of patterns, for which they claim to apply in day or short-term trading.

The *percentage of profitable trades* shows the portion of the total number of trades that have generated a profit. In the context of day and short-term trading performance analysis this is a very important parameter and may be viewed as the probability of the future success rate of a pattern. It is therefore required that this number be as high as possible, much higher than its theoretical minimum value of 50%. The minimum acceptable number depends on the *ratio of average winning to average losing trade*. For a ratio near unity, as it is often the case when the profit target equals the stop-loss, the minimum number recommended, by experience, is no less that 60% and that increases as the aforementioned ratio decreases. The theoretical formula is:

$$\%P > 100 / (R_{WL} + 1) \qquad\qquad (4\text{-}1)$$

This insures that the pattern will always produce a net profit. However, in order to get high probability patterns, an empirical formula is as follows:

$$\%P > 100 / (0.5625 * R_{wL} + 1) \qquad\qquad (4\text{-}2)$$

And it applies for values of R_{WL} less or equal to 1, which corresponds to the cases when the profit target is less or equal to the stop-loss. In those cases, the requirement for a much higher number of percent winners allows for the lower robustness that patterns with low average win to loss ratio exhibit. The practical reason for this is that a false or mistaken trading signal can affect real performance dramatically, as losers are much higher in value than winners. For values of the ratio much higher than one, it is recommended to maintain the 50% minimum requirement.

The *ratio of average winning to average losing trade*, $R_{wL,}$ is another very important parameter in short-term and day trading systems. It is calculated using two separate averages: one for all the winning trades and the other for all the losing trades. A low value for this ratio, below 1.0, means that, on average, losing trades are higher in absolute value than winning trades. The opposite is true when the value of the ratio is much higher than 1.0. In short-term and day trading, the value for this ratio is directly related to the profit target and stop-loss values set. Although trades do not always lose an amount indicated by the stop-loss due to conditions such as price gaps and fast markets, in the long term, this tends to be counter-balanced by higher profits gained due to favorable price gap openings. Commission size also affects the values of this ratio to a certain extent since they are subtracted from winning trades but added to losing trades.

Trend following systems tend to exhibit very high R_{wL} values because, by design, they have many small losing trades and very few but big winners. Therefore, their profitability, %P, can be small, as it can be seen using formula 4-1. For instance, if the ratio is equal to 4.0 then the system can be 20% profitable and still generate a profit.

In short-term trading it is recommended to use patterns with a ratio equal or even higher to 1.0. In this way, long term profitability can be maintained at a reasonably high percent profitability number, %P, in the range of 60 to 70%. For this purpose, the profit target must be selected to be equal or higher than the stop-loss.

The same holds true for day trading patterns, although in this case, in order to obtain high percent profitability it may be necessary to set stop-loss values higher than the profit targets values. This is true since intraday moves are smaller in comparison but still as volatile. It is recommended that patterns selected in this case have a much higher percent profitability, %P, according to formula 4-2. For instance, it can be seen from the equation that for a ratio equal to 0.5, the percent profitability required must be higher than 78%. That corresponds to cases when the profit target is half the stop-loss.

From the above discussion and from the formulas 4-1 and 4-2, it is evident that the parameters %P and R_{wL} are closely related, in a inverse manner. Obtaining profitable, high probability patterns requires a careful consideration of the values of these parameters.

The *maximum number of consecutive losers*, C_L, is another very important parameter in the performance analysis of patterns. It is found by looking at the detailed trade-by-trade historical analysis and finding the maximum number of consecutive losing trades. In general, it is desired that the value of this parameter is as low as possible. A value of zero would mean that the pattern, or system, is 100% profitable since no trades are losers. In practice, values between 1 and 5 are reasonable, depending on the number of trades, N. The reason for the dependence on N cornes form the fact that C_L can be an indication of how winners and losers are spaced over time. If a pattern has low N and big C_L then it means that most of the losers come in clusters and generate a high drawdown in comparison to the actual profit. When C_L is low and N is high, it means that the pattern generates good streaks of winners separated by a few losers, a very desirable performance. An empirical formula is as follows:

$$N > 10 \times C_L \qquad (4\text{-}3)$$

If, for instance, a pattern generates 5 consecutive losers, according to formula 4-3, then the number of trades must be greater than 50 to insure proper performance.

The *average time in a trade*, T_D, shows how many bars a trade lasts, on average. It is found by averaging the number of bars that each trade stays in an open position. Separate numbers may also be obtained for the winning and losing trades. While in trend following it is desired that this number is as high as possible for the winning trades, the opposite is true for short-term and day trading. In this case, the smallest possible number of one bar is the most desirable value. This would mean that winning trades exit on the same bar that the position was initiated (the next bar in the case when the position entry is at the close). This is a result of the short-term timing nature of these patterns. The longer they stay in a position, the higher may be the probability of a losing trade since patterns do not attempt to predict long term direction and trend. This also partly explains the vast difference between trend following and short-term trading system, both in philosophy and design.

The average time in a trade is also directly related to the profit target and stop-loss values. High values for these parameters result in trades staying open longer in order to either hit the profit target or stop-loss. Therefore, to obtain minimum T_D, it is necessary to select appropriate values for the profit target and stop-loss. The selection criteria must be based on the average volatility that the particular trading time frame and market exhibit. Short-term trading patterns must be selected to have a profit target and stop-loss level that falls within the range of short-term volatility. Day trading patterns must be selected on the basis of intraday volatility. There seems to be no rigid procedure for this selection but it depends on the particular market characteristics. For instance, for a stock with typical daily changes in the order of $2-$3, like Intel or Microsoft, patterns with profit target and stop-loss levels of the same order of magnitude will work better than, let us say, a pattern with $1 stop and profit levels. The latter will have a tendency to produce more losers since stops will tend to be hit more often than profit targets.

The *maximum drawdown*, D_R, refers to the maximum equity drop from a peak value. In short-term and day trading this parameter is directly related to the maximum number of consecutive losers, C_L. Also, in futures trading, this is one of the most important parameters and it is used to determine the capital size required trading a system. The same holds when trading marginable stocks. A more detailed discussion on this subject will be given in section three, in the money management chapter. For our purpose here, selection of patterns using the results of a performance analysis requires that the maximum drawdown is limited to a level equal to that of the consecutive losers. Higher drawdown would mean that the pattern does not operate uniformly over the analysis period, *i.e.* most of the losing trades occur during the same time period.

Table 4-3 gives a summary for the desired range of the values for the performance analysis parameters. The analysis period has also been included to note that a sufficiently long historical period is required to obtain valid results.

PARAMETER	DESIRED RANGE
Analysis Period	> 8 years
N	> 20 * bars in time frame
%P	> 60%
R_{WL}	≥ 1
C_L	< N/10
T_D	1 to 30 bars
D_R	$\leq C_L$ (in $)

TABLE 4-3: DESIRED RANGE FOR THE PERFORMANCE PARAMETERS

DATA REQUIREMENTS

Careful attention should be given to the type of historical data series used in the performance analysis of patterns. In general, there are two types of data series available: spilt adjusted and non-adjusted. Both types can be used if the appropriate provisions are taken to account for stock splits (and rarely for inverse stock splits). Use of split-adjusted data is popular since there are no price gaps in the data caused by stock splitting. However, unless proper adjustments are made to the testing program, these time series should only be used to study the general behavior of a pattern or trading system and not the actual price levels of entries and exits, since the latter may not correspond to actual prices. Furthermore, the use of price increments for the profit target and stop-loss must be carefully applied since some portion of this type of data does not correspond to actual price levels. To avoid complications, percentages may be used instead. If actual non-adjusted data is used, proper care should be exercised to adjust any open positions to account for splits. Most popular trading system back-testing packages allow for this type of adjustment.

MECHANICS OF BACK-TESTING STOCKS

Evidently, there are some notable differences in the process of back testing using stock data versus futures data. Futures involve a given contract size with a specific margin and the total profit is often reported on a unit contract traded basis. Usually, an initial trading capital per contract traded is established that covers margin plus expected drawdown. The return on the account is based on that initial trading capital. On the other hand, stocks do not have a given contract size and there is very little meaning to report profits per unit of stock traded, as well as establish a initial trading capital based on margin and drawdown.

In order to be able to make fair comparisons on the performance of patterns and trading systems for the stock market, it is necessary to normalize the results based on a standard measure. This standard measure is set here to be an initial trading capital equal to $1,000, which remains constant throughout the analysis period. What varies is the number of shares, S, bought or sold at every entry point, which is calculated according to the following formula:

$$S = \$1,000/\text{entry price}$$

Therefore, the number of shares will vary at every entry point depending on the entry price but the dollar amount used to initiate a position will remain the same.

An important advantage of the above method is that the level of risk assumed in each new trade is kept constant when using percentages for the profit target and stop-loss. This happens since at every entry a constant dollar amount of stock is bought. To illustrate this, let us consider a percent profit target T_P and a percent stop-loss T_S. Then, the dollar amount for the stop-loss is given by:

$$\begin{aligned} \$\,\text{Stop-Loss} &= \text{Number of Shares} \times \text{Entry price} \times T_S/100 \\ &= (\$1,000/\text{Entry price}) \times \text{Entry price} \times T_S/100 \\ &= 10 * T_S \end{aligned}$$

The final result shows that the number of shares, for a given account size, does not play any role in the risk assumed per trade, but only the stop-loss, T_S. Equivalently, the same holds true for the profit target and it can be easily shown that:

$$\$\,\text{Profit target} = 10 * T_P$$

Therefore, as a consequence, all performance analysis results in this book will be based on a constant dollar size entry as opposed to a constant number of shares and will utilize percentage profit targets and stop-losses.

If one elects to make a performance analysis based on a constant unit of stock traded then, as compared to using a constant dollar size, the total number of trades, N, the percent profitable trades, %P and the maximum number of consecutive losers, C_L, will be the same and can be compared directly. However, all other parameters, such as the ratio of average win to average loss, R_{WL} and the maximum drawdown, D_R will be different in actual value and therefore the performance of different patterns cannot be compared directly based on those.

EXAMPLE 1: THE GAMMA PATTERN

The Gamma pattern is a very simple chart formation that involves only the closes of four consecutive daily bars. It can be used to take long positions in many stocks. Figure 4-1 shows a graphical description of this pattern. The bar sequence is as follows:

$$S = \{(C_0), (C_1), (C_2), (C_3)\}$$

The pattern has a length equal to four daily bars. The trading rules are as follows:

If C[2] > C[1] and C[1] > C[0] and C[0] > C[3] then
Buy S number of shares tomorrow on the open with
profit target at entry price x $(1 + T_P/100)$ and
stop-loss at entry price x $(1 - T_S/100)$

where: S = \$1,000/entry price
and: T_P and T_S numbers greater than 0.

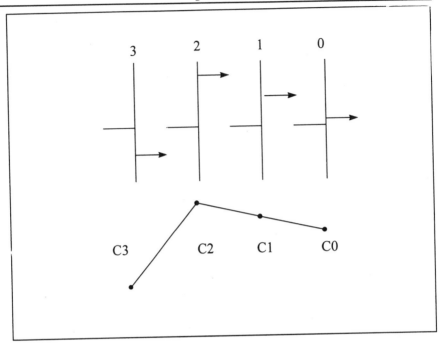

FIGURE 4-1: THE GAMMA PATTERN

Table 4-4 shows the testing results for Microsoft (MSFT) for the period of 1/1990 to 1/2000 using split-adjusted data and a profit target and stop-loss equal to 7%. The Gamma pattern is 65.75% profitable and generates 73 trades. The ratio of average winning to average losing trade is 1.05, as expected near unity, and the number of consecutive losers equal to 5, less than the maximum number given by formula 4-3. The return on the account of $1,000 is 121%, a number that in reality is sensitive to other factors, as it is also the case with all dollar figures in the table. These factors include, but not limited to:

1. The actual entry price as compared to the open price
2. The actual order size as compared to the estimated, S
3. Partially filled orders.
4. Actual commission paid.

The effect of the above factors cannot be approximated in the testing. However, the fourth column of the table that includes the percent profitable trades and the number of trades generated will not be seriously affected by those factors. Here, the reader should understand that every analysis involves certain assumptions in order to be made possible to carry out. It is therefore important for the reader to know those assumptions, although it is often the case in the literature that the assumptions made are not disclosed.

Table 4-5 shows the testing results for the Gamma pattern for AT&T Corporation (T). Again, a profit target and stop-loss of 7% were used. The pattern is 69.70% profitable with a ratio of average win to average loss of 0.95 and generates 33 trades. The maximum number of consecutive losers is three, which is within the acceptable range.

Table 4-6 shows the testing results for the Gamma patterns for Intel Corp. (INTC). For a profit target and stop-loss of 6% the pattern gain is 67.80% profitable with 59 trades generated. The maximum number of consecutive losers is 4, below the maximum allowable value. The ratio of average winning to average losing trade is 0.95.

At this point a natural question would involve the sensitivity of the Gamma pattern to various profit targets and stop-loss levels. This is shown on Table 4-7 where the profitability of the pattern for the three different stocks tested is calculated as a function of the profit target and stop-loss level.

Percent $T_P = T_S$	MSFT	T	INTC
3	53	60	60
4	60	60	61
5	63	57	64
6	65	63	68
7	66	70	60
8	66	59	59
9	65	61	61
10	68	61	58

TABLE 4-7: GAMMA PATTERN PROFITABILITY

It may be seen (Table 4-7) that for an equal profit target and stop-loss ranging from 3 to 10, the profitability of the Gamma pattern is well above 50% for all three stocks. This implies a robustness of the pattern performance to these parameters.

TradeStation Strategy Performance Report - Gamma MSFT-Daily (1/2/90-1/31/00)

Performance Summary: All Trades

Total Net Profit	$1,209.45	Open position P/L	$0.00
Gross Profit	$2,409.59	Gross Loss	($1,200.14)
Total # of trades	73	Percent profitable	65.75%
Number winning trades	48	Number losing trades	25
Largest winning trade	$132.11	Largest losing trade	($72.77)
Average winning trade	$50.20	Average losing trade	($48.01)
Ratio avg win/avg loss	1.05	Avg trade (win & loss)	$16.57
Max consec. Winners	12	Max consec. losers	5
Avg # bars in winners	5	Avg # bars in losers	4
Max intraday drawdown		($378.80)	
Profit Factor	2.01	Max # contracts held	791

TABLE 4-4: THE GAMMA PATTERN PERFORMANCE FOR MSFT

TradeStation Strategy Performance Report - Gamma T-Daily
(1/2/90-1/31/00)

Performance Summary - All Trades

Total Net Profit	$900.17	Open position P/L	$0.00
Gross Profit	$1,658.44	Gross Loss	($758.27)
Total # of trades	33	Percent profitable	69.70%
Number winning trades	23	Number losing trades	10
Largest winning trade	$85.25	Largest losing trade	($120.91)
Average winning trade	$72.11	Average losing trade	($75.83)
Ratio avg win/avg loss	.95	Avg trade (win & loss)	$27.28
Max consec. Winners	11	Max consec. losers	3
Avg # bars in winners	25	Avg # bars in losers	25
Max intraday drawdown		($261.88)	
Profit Factor	2.19	Max # contracts held	66

TABLE 4-5: THE GAMMA PATTERN PERFORMANCE FOR AT&T

TradeStation Strategy Performance Report - Gamma INTC-Daily
(1/2/90-1/31/00)

Performance Summary: All Trades

Total Net Profit	$1,311.05	Open position P/L	$0.00
Gross Profit	$2,616.45	Gross Loss	($1,305.40)
Total # of trades	59	Percent profitable	67.80%
Number winning trades	40	Number losing trades	19
Largest winning trade	$84.07	Largest losing trade	($101.72)
Average winning trade	$65.41	Average losing trade	($68.71)
Ratio avg win/avg loss	95	Avg trade (win & loss)	$22.22
Max consec. Winners	7	Max consec. losers	4
Avg # bars in winners	8	Avg # bars in losers	7
Max intraday drawdown		($347.72)	
Profit Factor	2.00	Max # contracts held	386

TABLE 4-6: THE GAMMA PATTERN PERFORMANCE FOR INTEL

EXAMPLE 2: THE LAMBDA PATTERN

The Lambda pattern is another very simple chart formation that involves just the closes of four consecutive daily bars. It can be used to take short positions in many stocks. Figure 4-2 shows a graphical description of this pattern. The bar sequence is as follows:

$$S = \{(C_0), (C_1), (C_2), (C_3)\}$$

The pattern has a length equal to four daily bars. The trading rules are:

If C[3] > C[0] and C[0] > C[1] and C[1] > C[2] then
Sell S number of shares tomorrow on the open with
profit target at entry price x $(1 - T_P / 100)$ and
stop-loss at entry price x $(1 + T_S / 100)$

where: S = $1,000/entry price
and: T_P and T_S numbers greater than 0.
Table 4-8 shows the testing results for Apple Computer (AAPL) for the period of 1/1990 to 01/2000 using split-adjusted data and a profit target and stop-loss-equal to 6%. The Lambda pattern is 62% profitable and generates 52 trades. The ratio of average winning to average losing trade is unity as expected and the number of consecutive losers equal to 3, less than the maximum number given by formula 4-3. We may also mention that the return on the account of $1,000 is 75%.

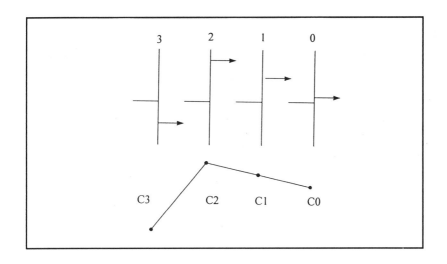

FIGURE 4-2: THE LAMBDA PATTERN

TradeStation Strategy Performance Report - Lambda AAPL-Daily (1/2/90-1/31/00)

Performance Summary: All Trades

Total Net Profit	$753.83	Open position P/L	$0.00
Gross Profit	$1,980.20	Gross Loss	($1,226.37)
Total # of trades	52	Percent profitable	61.54%
Number winning trades	32	Number losing trades	20
Largest winning trade	$89.25	Largest losing trade	($74.38)
Average winning trade	$61.88	Average losing trade	($61.32)
Ratio avg win/avg loss	1.01	Avg trade (win & loss)	$14.50
Max consec. Winners	10	Max consec. losers	3
Avg # bars in winners	6	Avg # bars in losers	6
Max intraday drawdown		($197.92)	
Profit Factor	1.61	Max # contracts held	63

TABLE 4-8: THE LAMBDA PATTERN PERFORMANCE FOR APPLE COMPUTER

SECTION TWO

DISCOVERING STOCK PATTERNS

The successful application of trading systems in day or short-term trading based on price patterns requires generating a large number of entry points and corresponding exit points. This translates directly into the need for a presence of a large number of price patterns. Discovering the patterns is the task of a *pattern searching process*. This type of process can prove to be a very tedious and time-consuming exercise. Historical data must be carefully analyzed and pattern candidates must be singled out for subsequent back-testing and analysis. This must be repeated for several different securities. Furthermore, it must also be repeated in regular time intervals, in the future, as more data is being collected.

In this section, techniques for discovering patterns are discussed. These techniques range from a visual inspection, suitable to the beginner, to automatic search techniques utilizing advanced algorithms, for those that are more advanced. My intention is to introduce the reader to these concepts and provide a foundation for further development rather than to hand out specific algorithms and code that does the job.

Those that would like to concentrate only on the practical aspects of using the patterns listed in section four can skip this section and go directly to section three.

CHAPTER FIVE

VISUAL SEARCH TECHNIQUES

The simplest way of discovering price patterns is by looking at stock charts and trying to identify those formations that have a good probability to generate profits in the future. This type of visual inspection technique is the most common method used by many traders. Depending on the experience level and ability to analyze charts, one may be able to identify profitable patterns. Some of the patterns found by this process might be more profitable than others. Although this is essentially a trial-and-error method, it is still legitimate. However, unless a systematic framework is present for implementing and executing such a method of discovering patterns, the chances of long-term consistent profitability are very small.

Figure 5-1 shows a systematic approach to the visual searching for patterns and the steps required to transform this simple technique into a powerful trading tool:

69

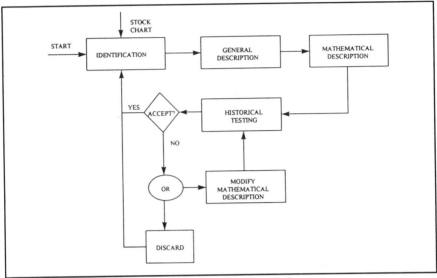

FIGURE 5-1: VISUAL SEARCH PROCEDURE

IDENTIFICATION:

In the visual inspection method, the identification of a pattern is mainly based on the ability of the stock chart examiner to spot familiar price bar formations that in the past have known to produce satisfactory results. This is a step that assumes a certain level of experience with chart analysis. One may have noticed, for instance, that whenever the stock price has made three consecutive closes below the low of each previous bar then the forth close was above the high of the third bar. When three consecutive bars on the chart are found satisfying this condition then a pattern has been identified.

It is also possible that pattern identification be based on an arbitrary selection of a candidate pattern. Although this is a legitimate way of discovering patterns, it is much more time consuming and tedious, as compared with identification based on previous experience of market behavior. Nevertheless, arbitrary pattern formations can be singled out from stock charts and considered for further evaluation. This method has worked for many traders in the past, including the author, and especially for beginners who do not have great exposure to the market.

Irrespectively of the method used and the ability to visually spot pattern formations, it is necessary that those found produce a timely move of appropriate magnitude in the desired direction. It is important to note that the objective here is not to identify patterns that mark major market turning points. The longer-term direction of the market is irrelevant in short-term or day trading. Therefore, one should not be influenced by the market trend, if any, when selecting pattern candidates. Prices may be trending up but a pattern that generates good profits for short positions may be forming. Conversely, prices may be trending down but one may be possible to spot a good pattern for taking long positions.

GENERAL DESCRIPTION:

After a pattern has been identified it is important to understand how it functions, so it can then be implemented and its performance analyzed. This step facilitates easier implementation of the pattern logic for subsequent performance evaluation. One way to achieve this is to isolate the pattern from the chart and attempt to describe its operation in simple language.

One of the basic problems in implementing a pattern is to decide which parameters to include in its mathematical description. This interim step of a general description assists in this process.

An example of a general description is as follows:

1. The pattern looks like a reversal made up of four bars.
2. The close of the third bar is below the low of the second.

3. The high of the last bar is above the close of the first.
4. The low of the third bar looks like a short-term bottom.

And so on...

The more insight into the pattern structure that can be obtained from this step, the easier it will be getting a mathematical description and a final assessment on whether the pattern can be used in trading. As more experience is gained in dealing with this step, the more efficient and meaningful it becomes.

MATHEMATICAL DESCRIPTION:

Getting a mathematical description for a pattern is necessary in order to proceed with a historical analysis of its performance. This "modeling" step requires deriving an exact mathematical description of the pattern formation. Fuzzy descriptions may be useful in another context but are of no real use when the exact timing of entry signals is a priority, such as in the case of day and short-term trading.

The mathematical descriptions of price patterns are often very simple and most often account for few simple comparisons of the basic parameters that describe the bars that form the pattern, *i.e.* the high, low, open and close. This is a distinct advantage over other technical trading methods that involve complicated mathematical operations and formulas.

One problem that may arise during this step is to decide which of the bar parameters to include in the pattern logic. Unfortunately, besides the trial-and-error method, I cannot suggest anything else for the visual technique. As one becomes more experienced with patterns and their analysis, then it may be easier to decide in a more efficient manner.

An example of a mathematical description, or "model" is:

$$C[1] < L[2] \text{ and } H[0] > C[4] \text{ and } L[3] < L[2]$$

where the C stands for the close, the H for the high and L for the low. The index in the parenthesis denoted the bar number in the pattern formation, as was explained in chapter 2.

The above describes only a pattern and it is not a complete and useful trading model, as this would further require the inclusion of specific entry and exit rules and appropriate money management.

HISTORICAL TESTING:

The objective of this step is to determine the past performance of a pattern discovered. In order to achieve that the pattern mathematical description must be first combined with a profit target and stop-loss of appropriate magnitude. Then, the historical performance can be obtained by either writing software code or using a trading system back-testing software package. The latter is a much faster and efficient way of getting the job done, as most of the work for accomplishing it is done in a high level-computing environment that requires minimal input from the user. However, some basic knowledge of the principles of computer modeling and back-testing works is required, along with a programming skill. If someone is unfamiliar in using these software programs, (and I can mention here one, without making any specific endorsement, the TradeStation by Omega Research, Inc.), then there will be a learning curve lasting anywhere from three months to a full year, depending on the user's background and experience. Attending a demo session on how these packages work, or even going to a seminar and spending some time with the experts can often prove to be time well spent that can add good value to a trader's job.

If the results of the historical analysis step are acceptable then the process may be repeated for other patterns. If the results are unacceptable then the pattern can either be discarded or an attempt made to improve its performance.

MODIFY MATHEMATICAL DESCRIPTION:

In this step, the parameters included in the pattern mathematical description are reconsidered and a decision is made whether to include some new and/or omit some of the existing. Experience has shown that modification of a pattern mathematical description can result in a major improvement only if the performance already available is, at least, marginal. Therefore, the objective of this step must be to improve performance rather than to turn it around from negative to positive.

There can be no specific guidelines for this step other than to say that it is basically a trial-and-error procedure. Again, as one becomes more experienced with this process, the more efficient it becomes.

VISUAL SEARCH EXAMPLE: THE THREE-LOW REVERSAL PATTERN, 3L-R

As an example of the visual search for patterns, let us consider the daily bar chart of General Motors (GM) shown in figure 5-2. By examining the chart, one may notice that around June 24, 1999 the stock made a short- term bottom at about $61 per share but then moved up about $12 in a week's time. It is possible then that a price pattern was formed at that short-term bottom that gave a signal for a long position.

GENERAL DESCRIPTION:

One may start by noticing that the low made on June 24, 1999 was lower than the low of the previous day. Also, the previous day low was lower than the low of the day before it. Then, a lower low was made for two days in a row. Therefore, there are two consecutive new daily lows, which can be part of the pattern logic. The day following the lowest low, the prices reversed with a daily high above the high of the first bar in the pattern and then closed above the high of the second day in the pattern. The four daily bars that form the candidate pattern are enclosed in a box in figure 5-2.

Due to the behavior of prices in the candidate pattern, I call this the 3L-R pattern, standing for a three day low followed by a reversal.

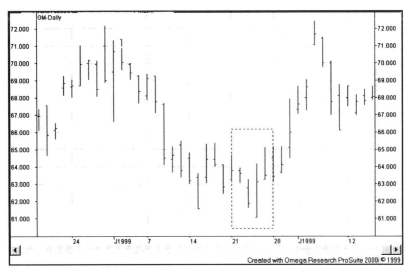

FIGURE 5-2: IDENTIFYING A PATTERN BY VISUAL SEARCH

MATHEMATICAL DESCRIPTION:

Only four daily bars make up this pattern formation. One first choice for the pattern logic is selected to be as follows:

Low of yesterday is lower than the low of 2 days ago and
Low of 2 days ago is lower than the low of 3 days ago and
Close of today is higher than the high of 2 days ago

The above may be represented in mathematical form as follows:

$$L[1] < L[2] \text{ and } L[2] < L[3] \text{ and } C[0] > H[2]$$

where the "L's" stand for the lows, the "H" for the high and the "C's" for the closes. The indexes in the parentheses stand for the corresponding bar number, starting at 0 for the last bar in the pattern formation considered.

The bar sequence, S, for the pattern is as follows:

$$S = \{ (C_0), (L_1), (L_2, H_2), (L_3) \}$$

A graphical representation of the pattern is shown in figure 5-3a. Again, only the quantities labeled with arrows are included in the pattern logic. The remaining quantities are of no interest and their relative position can be anywhere. Therefore, the graphical representation of the pattern 3L-R in figure 5-3a shows only one possible version of it when one considers all of the parameters of the bars.

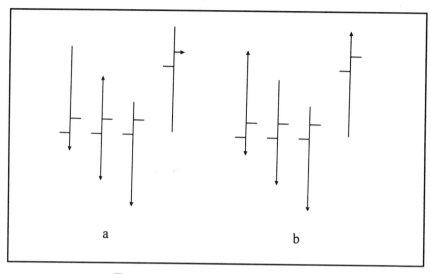

FIGURE 5-3: THE 3L-R PATTERN

HISTORICAL TESTING:

Historical testing, or back-testing, requires that a complete trading system model that includes the mathematical logic of the pattern together with the appropriate risk control parameters is available.

In the case of the 3L-R pattern discussed above the trading system model may be defined as follows:

If L[1] < L[2] and L[2] < L[3] and C[0] > H[2] Then
Buy tomorrow on the open with
Profit target at entry price * (1 + Tp/100)
Protective stop at entry price * (1-Ts/100)

Where:

Tp is the percent profit target and Ts the percent stop-loss.

Table 5-1 shows the back-testing results for General Motors (GM). The test period is from 01/1990 to 01/2000, the profit target and stop-loss are set to 7%. The performance results indicate a 67.57% profitable system with acceptable levels for the remaining parameters.

MODIFY MATHEMATICAL DESCRIPTION:

The pattern logic is now modified to determine if there is a significant change in the performance of the trading system model. For that purpose, the high of the last bar in the pattern formation is compared to the high of the first bar, as follows:

Low of yesterday is lower than the low of 2 days ago and
Low of 2 days ago is lower than the low of 3 days ago and
High of today is higher than the high of 3 days ago

The above may be represented in mathematical form as follows:

L[1] < L[2] and L[2] < L[3] and H[0] > H[3]

The "L's" stand for the lows and the "H" for the high. Note that in this case there is no reference to any of the closes. The indexes in the parentheses stand for the corresponding bar number, starting at 0 for the last bar in the pattern formation considered.

The bar sequence, S, for the pattern is as follows:

$$S = \{ (H_0), (L_1), (L_2), (H_3, L_3) \}$$

A graphical representation of the pattern is shown in figure 5-3b. Again, only the quantities labeled with arrows are included in the pattern logic. The remaining quantities are of no interest and their relative position with respect to themselves and the

78

labeled quantities can be anywhere. Therefore, the graphical representation of the pattern 3L-R in figure 5-3b shows only one possible version of it when one considers all of the parameters of the bars.

REPEAT HISTORICAL TESTING:

The new trading system model may be defined as follows:

If L[1] < L[2] and L[2] < L[3] and H[0] > H[3] Then
Buy tomorrow on the open with
Profit target at entry price * (1 + Tp/100)
Protective stop at entry price * (1-Ts/100)

Where:

Tp is the percent profit target and Ts the percent stop-loss.

Table 5-2 shows the new testing results for General Motors (GM). The test period is gained from 01/1990 to 01/2000 and the profit target and stop-loss are set 7%. The performance results indicate a 70% profitable system while some parameters are improved, as compared with the results of table 5-1. Specifically, the ratio of average win to average loss is just above unity and the return on account has increased. The only parameter that has changed adversely is the drawdown but this change is not very significant.

One may continue modifying the pattern logic and then repeating the back testing. This is left as an exercise to the reader.

The 3L-R pattern can be used to trade several stocks, or even futures. A list of stocks and the associated historical performance of the pattern is given in the pattern library of section 4.

TradeStation Strategy Performance Report - 3L-R GM-Daily
(1/2/90-1/4/00)

Performance Summary: All Trades

Total Net Profit	$956.40	Open position P/L	($12.19)
Gross Profit	$1,798.63	Gross Loss	($842.22)
Total # of trades	37	Percent profitable	67.57%
Number winning trades	25	Number losing trades	12
Largest winning trade	$98.45	Largest losing trade	($72.36)
Average winning trade	$71.95	Average losing trade	($70.19)
Ratio avg win/avg loss	1.03	Avg trade (win & loss)	$25.85
Max consec. Winners	5	Max consec. losers	2
Avg # bars in winners	15	Avg # bars in losers	19
Max intraday drawdown		($187.69)	
Profit Factor	2.14	Max # contracts held	7

TABLE 5-1: THE 3L-R PATTERN PERFORMANCE FOR GENERAL MOTORS

TradeStation Strategy Performance Report - 3L-R GM-Daily
(1/2/90-1/4/00)

Performance Summary: All Trades

Total Net Profit	$1,178.27	Open position P/L	($12.19)
Gross Profit	$2,018.25	Gross Loss	($839.98)
Total # of trades	40	Percent profitable	70.00%
Number winning trades	28	Number losing trades	12
Largest winning trade	$98.45	Largest losing trade	($72.36)
Average winning trade	$72.08	Average losing trade	($70.00)
Ratio avg win/avg loss	1.03	Avg trade (win & loss)	$29.46
Max consec. Winners	7	Max consec. losers	2
Avg # bars in winners	17	Avg # bars in losers	8
Max intraday drawdown		($196.73)	
Profit Factor	2.40	Max # contracts held	36

TABLE 5-2: THE 3L-R PATTERN PERFORMANCE FOR GENERAL MOTORS
- MODIFIED DESCRIPTION

Chapter Six

Automatic Pattern Search

In chapter 5, I described a procedure for discovering patterns based on a visual inspection of stock charts. In reality though, this type of tedious and time consuming exercise is only worth the effort spent when viewed as a training exercise in system modeling and back-testing. In order to accomplish anything of significance that can provide a competitive advantage, one has to develop a more efficient and productive means of searching stock charts and discovering price patterns.

The motivation for the Automatic Pattern Search, (APS), procedure comes from the simple realization that the process of visual searching can be emulated in the computer. In fact, computers are better suited than humans are at handling these type of tedious and repetitive tasks. They can do this in a faster and more efficient manner. As processor speeds get faster, the implementation and execution of large-scale "data mining" techniques becomes more feasible. Data mining is that subject of computational mathematics that deals with the identification of patterns hidden in all sorts of data files. The automatic pattern search methods I describe in this chapter fall under this general subject but are customized to apply to historical data for stocks and the price patterns that form in it.

81

Two different methods to search for profitable patterns are introduced in this chapter: the Combinatorial Pattern Formation method (CPF) and the Exhaustive Pattern Search method (EPS). These two methods allow for *a priori*, identification of patterns. This is in contrast to the method presented in chapter 7, the Daily Pattern Identification (DPI), where the pattern identification is based on a *posterior* means, *i.e.* by waiting for it to form first.

The discussions that follow are by no means an in-depth treatment of the subject. Doing this would probably require a separate and very computationally heavy publication. The objective here is to provide the reader with the necessary framework and foundation needed to proceed in applying the concepts presented.

THE COMBINATORIAL PATTERN FORMATION METHOD (CPF)

This method is based on generating a vast universe of possible pattern formations that could form in stock data and then checking to see which ones exist in the historical data of a stock while satisfying a set of desired performance criteria. The pattern universe is generated in advance and is independent of any particular stock being considered. In order to generate this pattern universe, combinatorial analysis must be used in conjunction with the pattern types discussed in chapter 4. This universe can, at least theoretically, get as large as one wishes it to be.

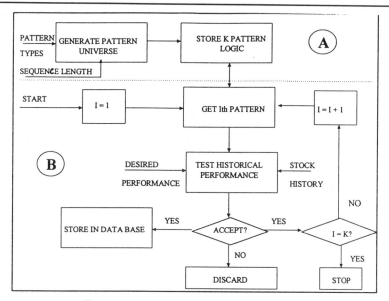

FIGURE 6-1: THE CPF METHOD

Figure 6-1 illustrates the CPF method in block diagram form. There are two stages to this method, A and B, as shown in the diagram and separated by the dotted line.

Stage A is the formation of the pattern universe. The inputs to this stage are the pattern types considered and the maximum bar sequence lengths. The procedure for generating the pattern formations is based on combinatorial analysis. When all the pattern formations are generated, k in number, they are properly indexed and stored in a database.

In stage B, all the patterns found in stage A are back-tested to determine which ones satisfy a set of desired performance criteria. This is like a filter stage. It works sequentially, by taking each pattern formation from the database of stage A and testing its performance using data for a specific stock. If the performance is acceptable then the pattern is stored in a database of acceptable patterns and the process is repeated for the next pattern in line. If the performance is not acceptable, the pattern is discarded.

The CPF method has certain advantages and disadvantages over other search methods.

ADVANTAGES:

1. Choice of the mix and size of the universe
2. Execution times of stage B can be estimated in advance
3. Allows parallel processing

DISADVANTAGE:

1. Stage A generates many useless patterns

The size of the database of stage A can be controlled by varying the number of pattern types considered and the maximum bar sequence length. As soon as all the pattern combinations are generated — and this is done only once — the time necessary to back-test them can be estimated. Furthermore, as long as the database of pattern formations is present, any number of stocks can be tested using a parallel architecture. This can reduce the time required to test a high number of issues significantly.

The drawback of this method is that stage A generates a large number of useless pattern formations that may never appear in stock data. There is a trade-off present there but as one gets more experienced with the process, the combinatorial analysis can be adjusted to generate useful pattern formations.

A typical database generated by the CPF method may include anywhere from 100,000 to 1,000,000 patterns. Calculating the historical performance of such a high number of patterns can take many hours or even several days, depending on the size of the database and processor speeds. However, this is a process that can run in the background and the resulting good patterns found can then be used in trading. Furthermore, the method is applicable to both daily and intraday data.

EXAMPLES OF THE CPF METHOD

SINGLE BAR PATTERNS

The best way to illustrate how the CPF method works, especially stage A is by a few examples. For this purpose, let us first consider the trivial case where the bar sequence length in stage A of the CPF method shown in figure 6-1 is set to one. This means that all the patterns to be generated are made of just a single bar.

In the case of the exact patterns type, as defined in chapter 3, the pattern formation combinations to be generated are those of all the possible forms of a price bar. These possibilities were described in chapter two (see figure 2-2). There are twelve combinations in total for the bar sequence that is defined as:

$$S = \{(O,H,L,C)\}$$

And include those cases where some of the quantities in the bar are equal.

Therefore, in this trivial case, there are 12 exact pattern formations to store in the database. Those are:

1. $C < H$ and $C > O$ and $O > L$
2. $C = H$ and $C > O$ and $O > L$
3. $C < H$ and $C > O$ and $O = L$
4. $C = H$ and $C > O$ and $O = L$
5. $C = H$ and $O = H$ and $H > L$
6. $O < H$ and $O > C$ and $C > L$
7. $O < H$ and $O > C$ and $C = L$
8. $O = H$ and $O > C$ and $C > L$
9. $O = H$ and $O > C$ and $C = L$
10. $O = L$ and $C = L$ and $H > L$
11. $O = C$ and $C < H$ and $O > L$
12. $O = C$ and $H = L$ and $C = L$

Please note that there are only two cases, 1 and 6, that do not involve any ties.

If we further consider split pattern formations, then the pattern type is given as:

$$P = S\{E\{S_1\}, E\{S_2\}\}$$

And in this trivial case of a single bar, patterns can be described as:

$$P = S\{E\{(O_1,H_1,L_1,C_1)\}, E\{(O_2,H_2,L_2,C_2)\}\}$$

By definition, this split pattern is made of two price bars where each price bar stands for a pattern and there is not any comparison to be made between the parameters of the two bars. Therefore, there are a total of 144 combinations of formation (12 X 12), or split patterns. This increases the universe of our pattern formations to 156 (12 exact + 144 split). If equalities are excluded, the pattern universe is reduced to just 6 patterns (2 exact + 4 split). In this much simpler case, the 6 possible pattern formations are as follows:

1. $C_1 < H_1$ and $C_1 > O_1$ and $O_1 > L_1$
2. $O_1 < H_1$ and $O_1 > C_1$ and $C_1 > L_1$
3. $C_1 < H_1$ and $C_1 > O_1$ and $O_1 > L_1$ and $C_2 < H_2$ and $C_2 > O_2$ and $O_2 > L_2$
4. $C_1 < H_1$ and $C_1 > O_1$ and $O_1 > L_1$ and $O_2 < H_2$ and $O_2 > C_2$ and $C_2 > L_2$
5. $O_1 < H_1$ and $O_1 > C_1$ and $C_1 > L_1$ and $O_2 < H_2$ and $O_2 > C_2$ and $C_2 > L_2$
6. $O_1 < H_1$ and $O_1 > C_1$ and $C_1 > L_1$ and $O_2 < H_2$ and $O_2 > C_2$ and $C_2 > L_2$

The intention for the above example was to illustrate the stage A of the CPF method and it is of no practical use since the patterns generated have the trivial length of one bar.

PATTERNS OF FOUR DAILY CLOSES

In order to illustrate the concept for a more practical case of patterns, I consider a sub-universe of pattern formations that is generated by all exact patterns that have the following bar sequence:

$$S = \{(C_0),(C_1),(C_2),(C_3)\}$$

In general, the total number of combinations, M_k, for a pattern that has k quantities present in its bar sequence, is given by the formula:

$$M_k = k!$$

where: $k! = 1 \times 2 \times 3 \times ...x K$ (Called K factorial)

In the case that: $K = 4$, then:

$$M_k = k! = 1 \times 2 \times 3 \times 4 = 24$$

Therefore, there is a total of 24 pattern formation combinations for the above bar sequence made up of the 4 closes. This does not include "ties," *i.e.* those cases where some quantities in the bar sequence are equal. The Gamma and Lambda patterns described in the example section of chapter 4 are just two of the 24 combinations formed here.

Table 6-1 shows the exact pattern formation combinations for different bar sequence lengths when just the closes of the price bars are considered and no two quantities in any of the bars are equal in magnitude. It may be seen that even in this simple case of a bear sequence, the number of pattern formations can increase fast to more than 5,000. If these combinations are used alone to generate other pattern types, such as split, overlay and delay, for instance, the total number of available pattern formations can increase dramatically, just for this simple case of bar sequence.

Bar Sequence Length*	Combinations
2	2
3	6
4	24
5	120
6	720
7	5040
Total:	5912

* Bar Sequence includes only the closes

TABLE 6-1: EXACT PATTERN FORMATION COMBINATIONS

MORE COMPLICATED PATTERN FORMS

In the cases of bar sequences that involve any mix of the open, high, low and close of bars, there are at least five conditions that must be met for each of the bars of the generated patterns. Those are:

$$H_i \geq L_i$$
$$O_i \leq H_i$$
$$O_i \geq L_i \qquad \text{For all bars } i = 0, ..., l\text{-}1$$
$$C_i \geq L_i$$
$$C_i \leq H_i$$

The above conditions assure that the patterns formed comply with the restrictions set by the definition of a price bar, where the high is always greater or equal to the low and the open and close never outside of the bar length. These conditions serve to reduce dramatically the number of possible pattern formations.

As an example, let us consider the following bar sequence:

$$S = \{(H_0, L_0), (H_1, L_1)\}$$

There are 4 quantities in the sequence, so the total number of combinations is:

$$M_4 = 4! = 1 \times 2 \times 3 \times 4 = 24$$

However, there are also the following conditions to be met:

$$H_0 > L_0 \text{ and } H_1 > L_1$$

The above conditions greatly reduce the number of pattern formations, each by a factor of 2 (equalities are not considered). The only valid combinations are then 6 in total, as follows (See figure 6-2):

1. $H_1 > H_0$ and $L_0 > L_1$ (Inside bar)
2. $H_0 > H_1$ and $L_0 > L_1$ and $H_1 > L_0$
3. $H_1 > H_0$ and $L_1 > L_0$ and $H_0 > L_1$
4. $L_0 > H_1$ (Gap Up)
5. $L_1 > H_0$ (Gap Down)
6. $H_0 > H_1$ and $L_1 > L_0$ (Outside Bar)

When equalities are taken into account, the number of pattern formations increases significantly. In this case that would mean that the following conditions could also apply:

$$H_0 = L_0 \text{ and/or } H_1 = L_1$$

Patterns that do not include any ties tend be more preferable, since formations with ties tend to be very sensitive to errors in the data.

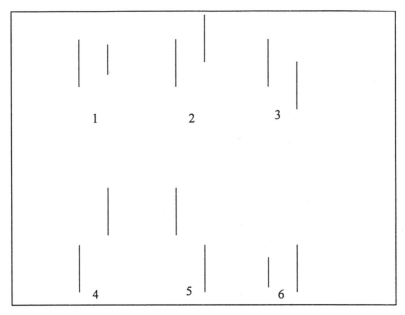

FIGURE 6-2: PATTERN COMBINATIONS OF TWO HIGH-LOW BARS

THE EXHAUSTIVE PATTERN SEARCH METHOD (EPS)

The CPF method presented in the previous section was based on *a priori* definition of a large universe of patterns and their subsequent historical testing to filter out those that generate acceptable performance results.

The EPS method tries to identify only the "good" patterns, by scanning historical data and storing the patterns that have satisfactory performance in a database. In this way, it avoids the time spent in testing useless pattern formations. The trade-off, however, is that the search must be repeated for each stock considered, whereas, in the CPF method, only the pattern evaluation is repeated.

The method can be applied by either walking forward or backward in the data, identifying the patterns formed in it and then testing their historical performance for the available data history.

The EPS method has certain advantages and disadvantages over other search methods, such as the CPF method:

ADVANTAGES:

1. Finds only the useful patterns
2. Minimal storage and disk access requirements

DISADVANTAGE:

1. A sequential processing method

Figure 6-3 shows the block diagram for this method. The search considers pattern formations with a maximum bar sequence length of l and a data file of historical data for a specific stock, containing N_b number of bars. The bars in the file are indexed starting from 1 up to N_b. The search starts with the first set of l consecutive bars in the file, which is used to identify the patterns formed in them according to the pattern types defined in advance. Those patterns, N_p in number, are then taken one at a time and their historical performance is analyzed to determine whether it satisfies a set of desired criteria. Those that satisfy the criteria are stored in a database and the remaining that do not are discarded. When all N_p patterns are tested, the search process continues by adding the next bar in the file at the end of the set of consecutive l bars and talking the last bar out. The new set is now used to identify the new N_p patterns formed in it which are in turn tested, one-by-one, to determine which ones are to be kept. The process terminates when all bars in the historical file of the stock have been taken into account in the search set of *l* bars length.

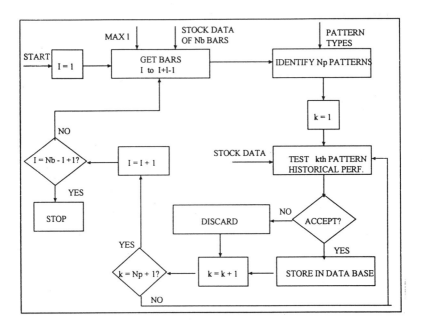

FIGURE 6-3: THE EPS METHOD

EXAMPLE OF THE EPS METHOD

The EPS method can best be described by an example. For this purpose, the method is applied to historical data of Intel Corporation (INTC) and a bar sequence of maximum 5 bars is considered (for simplicity). Let us also further assume that the search has progressed to the point in the data file that the first bar of the 5 bar sequence is exactly at the beginning of year 1999, specifically at 01/04/1999. The bars have the following dates:

Bar 5: 01/04/99   corresponding to: 0 in bar sequence
    4: 12/31/98   1
    3: 12/30/98   2
    2: 12/29/98   3
    1: 12/28/98   4

The chart formation is shown in figure 6-4. From all the pattern types available, just two are chosen, for illustration purposes: an exact pattern, P1, made up of the last three high-low bars and another exact, P2, made up of just the last four closes. The bar sequences of the patterns are:

S1 = {(H0 , L0) , (H1 ,L1) , (H2 , L2)}
S2 = {(C0) , (C1) , (C2) , (C3)}

The identification algorithm next determines the logic of the patterns based on the actual magnitudes of the corresponding quantities on the chart.

The logic for P1 is:

H[0] > H[2] and L[0] > L[1] and H[1] > L[0] and
L[1] > L[2] and H[2] > H[1]

The logic for P2 is:

C[0] > C[2] and C[2] > C[1] and C[3] > C[0]

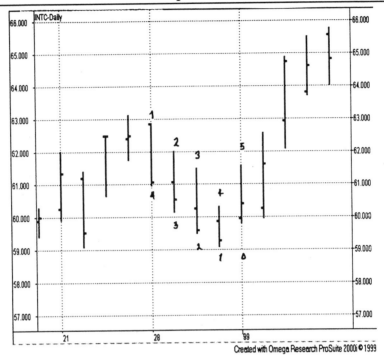

FIGURE 6-4: EPS METHOD EXAMPLE OF PATTERN FORMATION

The testing algorithm does not know in advance whether a pattern is suitable for long or short positions. Therefore, the pattern must be back-tested in both these two cases. In addition, a reasonable range of profit target and stop values must be used in determining the best applicable set. Lastly, in all cases, both the close of today and the open of next day may be used in the testing and the appropriate entry point selected according to the best performance.

The profit target and stop-loss may be varied according to:

$$Tps_{j+1} = Tps_j + 1 \; , \; Tps_0 = 1 \; , \; j = 0,1,2,3,\ldots,9$$
and
$$Tp_{j+1} = Ts_{j+1,} = Tps_{j+1}$$
where, Tp_{j+1} and Ts_{j+1} are the profit target and stop-loss in percentage terms, respectively, during test j+1. The profit target

equals the stop-loss in each test in order to obtain an average win to loss ratio as close to unity as possible. Using the above formula, both the profit target and stop-loss will range from 1% to 10%, which is sufficient for all practical cases.

Therefore, the historical testing procedure must consider the following:

1. Two patterns P1 and P2   (2)
2. Ten cases of profit targets and stops   (10)
3. Two different entry points (Open and close)   (2)
4. Two different signal cases (Long and Short)   (2)

The result above is a total of 80 tests, 40 tests for each pattern.

Tables 6-2 and 6-3 shows the back testing results of two out of the eighty cases. The details are as follows:

1. Two patterns P1 and P2
2. Profit Target = Stop-loss = 6%
3. Order entry at the Open of next day
4. Long signals only
5. Capital allocated per trade entry of $1,000
6. Test period: 01/1990 to 01/2000

Acceptance or rejection of the results in tables 6-2 and 6-3 may be best made according to a set of predefined criteria for the test values. These criteria may differ according to a trader's objectives but must conform to the general guidelines discussed in chapter 4. Therefore, according to set guidelines, pattern P1 is rejected immediately since the profitability is lower than the minimum recommended level of 60%. Pattern P2 may be retained or rejected depending on how strict the minimum profitability requirement is.

TradeStation Strategy Performance Report - P1 INTC-Daily (1/2/90-1/4/00)

Performance Summary: All Trades

Total Net Profit	$269.70	Open position P/L	$0.00
Gross Profit	$1,568.41	Gross Loss	($1,298.70)
Total # of trades	43	Percent profitable	55.81%
Number winning trades	24	Number losing trades	19
Largest winning trade	$95.76	Largest losing trade	($99.10)
Average winning trade	$65.35	Average losing trade	($68.35)
Ratio avg win/avg loss	.96	Avg trade (win & loss)	$6.27
Max consec. Winners	6	Max consec. losers	3
Avg # bars in winners	7	Avg # bars in losers	7
Max intraday drawdown		($322.30)	
Profit Factor	1.21	Max # contracts held	397

TABLE 6-2: HISTORICAL PERFORMANCE OF PATTERN P1 FOR INTC

TradeStation Strategy Performance Report - P2 INTC-Daily (1/2/90-1/4/00)

Performance Summary: All Trades

Total Net Profit	$1,060.19	Open position P/L	$0.00
Gross Profit	$2,682.66	Gross Loss	($1,622.47)
Total # of trades	63	Percent profitable	61.90%
Number winning trades	39	Number losing trades	24
Largest winning trade	$109.30	Largest losing trade	($98.12)
Average winning trade	$68.79	Average losing trade	($67.60)
Ratio avg win/avg loss	1.02	Avg trade (win & loss)	$16.83
Max consec. Winners	8	Max consec. losers	6
Avg # bars in winners	11	Avg # bars in losers	6
Max intraday drawdown		($365.52)	
Profit Factor	1.65	Max # contracts held	533

TABLE 6-3: HISTORICAL PERFORMANCE OF PATTERN P2 FOR INTC

CHAPTER SEVEN

DAILY PATTERN IDENTIFICATION

The Combinatorial Pattern Formation method (CPF) and the Exhaustive Pattern Search (EPS) method discussed in chapter 6 generate a data base of patterns that can be used to trade stocks short-term. The database may take longer to generate, several days or even weeks, due to the computationally intensive process involved in both methods. However, both methods may run in the background and do not interfere with the trading process. Furthermore, they can be applied both to daily and intraday data.

The Daily Pattern Identification (DPI) method concentrates only at those patterns that have formed in the last few days or bars. Essentially, this method is a limiting case of the EPS method where only the last few bars (most recent) in a data file are examined. It starts with an empty database, which is filled progressively, as more bars are added to the file and the method is re-applied.

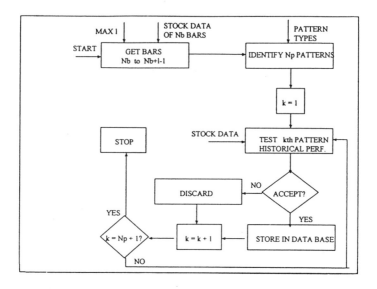

FIGURE 7-1: THE DPI METHOD

Figure 7-1 illustrates the DPI method. It starts by considering the last (most recent) l bars in a stock historical data file, where l is the maximum bar sequence length. Then, according to pattern types considered, N_p patterns are identified and their logic determined. The patterns are then back tested, one-by-one, and only those that satisfy a set of performance criteria are stored in a database.

When the method is first applied, the database is empty but it is gradually filled as more bars are added to the data file. In order for the method to generate a satisfactory number of patterns, it may need to run, on a daily basis, for a total of six months to a full year.

The DPI method has some advantages and disadvantages over the other pattern search methods:

ADVANTAGES:

1. Faster to execute
2. May be used in real-time for intraday trading
3. It is a means for calculating the p-Indicator

DISADVANTAGES:

1. Limits the entry point to that of the open of the next bar
2. Runs must be repeated daily

Obviously, the DPI method discussed here is a much faster method than either the CPF or EPS methods discussed in chapter 6. In essence, the DPI method is the last step of the EPS method, where only the last bar sequence of the stock historical data file is considered. Therefore, due to the faster execution, it may be implemented under real-time intraday conditions. In the case that the intraday price bars have a reasonable time period base, 15 or 30 minutes for instance, then there is enough time to identify and test patterns based on historical intraday data. Parallel processor architectures may best accomplish this task, where one processor is used to collect the real-time intraday data and the other to implement the DPI method.

Since the DPI method must wait for the next bar in the data file to be added — whether that is a daily or intraday bar — the method is not suitable for patterns that generate signals at the close of the last bar in the formation. This cuts the amount of historical testing that must be done by half, since now the identified patterns are only tested for an entry at the open of the next bar. However, in some cases, this also limits the number of profitable pattern formations that can be identified. Nevertheless, it is recommended to keep the close as an entry point and identify those profitable patterns that initiate trades on the close.

Those patterns may be useful in providing some indication on market direction. Also, In some cases where there is after-hours trading taking place during the time that the regular market is closed, the entry order can be executed with a delay in that session. If one is convinced that there is a good pattern or a set of good patterns that will generate profits then the order may be placed in that session even if the fill price is slightly worse than the expected entry price. In the long term, those variations are random effects that have a zero mean, there will also be cases that the fill will take place at a better price than expected.

Finally, in the case of short-term trading, the DPI method must be run daily or at every intraday bar, in the case of day trading. Although this can be totally automated, it still imposes a certain discipline burden on the part of the trader. The trade-off is, however, that it is a much faster method to execute.

EXAMPLE OF THE DPI METHOD

As mentioned before, the DPI method is the last step of the EPS method discussed in chapter six. Therefore, the same example presented in that case is also valid here. The assumption made here is that the date of 01/04/99, in the chart of figure 6-4, is the last day in the data file. Then, the identification and testing procedure is carried out exactly the same way as in the EPS method.

THE P-INDICATOR

The p-indicator is presented in this chapter since its calculation is a direct outcome of the DPI method.

In Technical Analysis, an indicator is mostly used to identify market trends, market direction and overbought/oversold conditions. Names such as the Relativity Strength Index (RSI), the Directional Movement Index (DMI), and Commodity Channel Index (CCI) come immediately to mind. Although Indicators are often used to time the markets, they fail to achieve that in the case of short-term and day trading with a high rate of success. The main reason is their time lag property; *i.e.* indicators always follow price action. This is implied mainly by their data averaging or smoothing properties. In the case of short-term trading, *i.e.* taking positions in the market that last a few days, most Indicators are not effective because they fail to predict short-term market direction. Some limited ability of a few indicators to follow trends is often overshadowed by the inability to timely predict sudden trend reversals, thus generating unacceptable drawdown. Nevertheless, the concept of looking at a single numerical quantity that ranges in value from 0 to 100, for instance, and generating trading signals based on that, is a very appealing one.

p-INDICATOR DEFINITION

The p-Indicator is a whole new concept in defining and constructing a technical analysis indicator. It is based on the use of short-term price patterns that are actually formed by the market price action. It is a short-term Indicator, only the last few days of a particular market are taken into account in the selection of the bar sequence length of the patterns considered in the Indicator. However, *the whole price history* of a particular security is considered when evaluating the past performance of those patterns. The theoretical range of values for the p-Indicator is from 0 to 100, but values between 30 and 70 are most common.

p-INDICATOR CALCULATION

The value of the p-Indicator is calculated as the sum of the percent profitability of each pattern considered weighted by the

number of occurrences of that pattern in the data history of a
security and divided by the sum of the occurrences of all patterns considered. Thus, the p-Indicator can be thought of as having two parts: one to be used for taking long positions and the
other for short positions. The calculation of each of the two parts
is identical but in the long part of the Indicator the historical
percent profitability of the patterns considered is calculated
based on taking long positions and in the short part based on
taking short positions.

The p-Indicator is calculated as follows:

Let: $i = 1, ..., N$ to be the number of pattern considered,

P_{Li} the percent profitability of each pattern for a long
position and P_{Si} for short,

T_i the number of "trades", or occurrences of the
pattern in the price history,

PI_L, the p-Indicator value for long position taking and
PI_S, for short. Then:

$$PI_L = \frac{\sum\limits_{i=1}^{N} P_{Li} T_i}{\sum\limits_{i=1}^{N} T_i} \qquad PI_S = \frac{\sum\limits_{i=1}^{N} P_{Si} T_i}{\sum\limits_{i=1}^{N} T_i}$$

PROPERTIES OF THE P-INDICATOR

CONSTRUCTION:

The p-Indicator resembles a weighted probability function. One may think of the historical profitability of a pattern as the probability that the next occurrence of that pattern has in giving a profitable signal. However, the more occurrences that a pattern has in the past, the more its historical profitability is weighted in the p-Indicator formula. To illustrate this with an example, let us assume the p-Indicator is made up of only three patterns. For each pattern the corresponding historical profitability, P_{Li}, is calculated for taking a long position. A specific profit target and protective stop is assumed in the calculations. The corresponding number of pattern occurrences is T_i. Let us further assume that the following hypothetical results are obtained:

$$P_1 = 65\% \quad T_1 = 120$$
$$P_2 = 85\% \quad T_2 = 65$$
$$P_3 = 40\% \quad T_3 = 225$$

The long portion of the p-Indicator is then:

$$PI_L = \frac{65 \times 120 + 85 \times 65 + 40 \times 225}{120 + 65 + 225} = 54.45\,\%$$

Thus, the new weighted profitability is 54.45 %, and that is the value of the p-Indicator for its long portion. Although P_1 and P_2 are 65% and 55% respectively, P_3, which is only 40%, greatly influences the final outcome because it is accompanied by a much higher number of pattern occurrences.

PRACTICAL USE OF THE INDICATOR:

When the value of PI_L is closer to 100, it indicates a better chance when taking a long position in the corresponding market. The reason for this is that most of the patterns considered in the calculation have a high profitability. Conversely, when the PI_S value is closer to 100, there is a better chance in taking short positions. In practice, numbers between 60 and 70 give good results. In short-term trading, the p-Indicator can be used as follows:

Long Position if: $PI_L > a,$ $a > 50$

Short Position if: $PI_S > b,$ $b > 50$

In addition, both long and short parts can be considered together as follows:

Long Position if: $PI_L > a$ and $PI_S < b,$ $a > 50$

Short Position if: $PI_L < b$ and $PI_S > a,$ $b < 50$

CALCULATION:

The determination of the values for the p-Indicator is a calculation intensive process. This is not very important when considering daily data but real-time calculations, if desired, can present a problem. Good results may be obtained by considering 10 different pattern formations, each for two different sets of profit targets and protective stops. For the resulting 20 patterns, the close of the day and the open of next day may be applied as the position entry, thus leaving a total of 40 patterns to be historically tested. In the case of daily data the calculation of the p-Indicator may take from several seconds to a few minutes, depending on processor speed.

The DPI method presented in this chapter provides a direct means for both discovering profitable price patterns and calculating the p-Indicator. All parameters necessary for this purpose are estimated at some stage of the method.

In summary, the following are needed:

1. The pattern formations
2. Each pattern's historical profitability and number of occurrences
3. The p-Indicator formula

CHARACTERISTICS:

It must be noted that when calculating the historical profitability of each pattern to be included in the p-Indicator formula, a profit target and a stop-loss of specific magnitude is taken into consideration. Thus, *the p-Indicator has the concept of profit target and stop-loss incorporated into its definition.* As far as I can know, this is the first and only technical Indicator with such a property that can be found in the literature. Its usefulness results from the fact that conventional Indicators generate entry signals for a particular market, long or short, but do not provide any indication whatsoever to the trader as to when to take profits or losses. With the p-Indicator, the profit or loss is known in advance, as soon as the signal is taken. In addition to that, the p-Indicator, at any given moment, *considers the whole price history in its calculations.* This is also the first time, as far as I know, that a trading Indicator has been developed with this inherent property.

In summary:

1. The p-Indicator has a built in profit target and protective stop.
2. Its calculation considers the whole price history of a security.

105

P-INDICATOR EXAMPLE

An example of the performance of the p-Indicator is presented here. The following trading system model is considered:

If $PI_L > a$ then buy at the open of tomorrow with
        Profit target at entry price * (1 + Tp/100)
        Protective stop at entry price * (1-Ts/100)
Where Tp and Ts are the percent profit target and stop-loss.

Tables 7-1 and 7-2 show the back-testing results for the p-Indicator for Microsoft (MSFT) and Intel (INTC) Corporations. Each test period is for 01/1996 to 01/2000. A daily data history from 01/1990 to 01/2000 is used to calculate the profitability and number of occurrences of the patterns included in the calculation of the indicator. The historical values of the indicator are then stored in two files called msft.his and intc.his. Therefore, although the historical testing starts at 01/96, there is sufficient history available so that the p-Indicator can be calculated (from 01/1990 to 01/1996 for the first record). As the testing progresses from the start date more bars are added to the test and the indicator calculations take those into account. The profit target was set equal to the stop-loss of 7% in the particular test. The variable a, in the trading model, was set to 62 for both tests in tables 7-1 and 7-2. A fixed dollar size of $1,000 was allocated to each new position.

Both tests (see tables 7-1 and 7-2) show the good performance of the p-Indicator. These test results are presented here as a demonstration of the p-Indicator capabilities only. Application of this indicator in real trading requires some practice with the parameters involved and selection of the applicable securities. As with most indicators, there may be some securities that it performs much better than others. Furthermore, adequate liquidity and market efficiency are necessary in order to obtain satisfactory performance, as is the case with all indicators.

TradeStation Strategy Performance Report - PIL MSFT.HIS-Daily (1/2/96-1/31/00)

Performance Summary: All Trades

Total Net Profit	$2,022.76	Open position P/L	($28.08)
Gross Profit	$3,994.12	Gross Loss	($1,971.37)
Total # of trades	97	Percent profitable	71.13%
Number winning trades	69	Number losing trades	28
Largest winning trade	$94.56	Largest losing trade	($78.01)
Average winning trade	$57.89	Average losing trade	($70.41)
Ratio avg win/avg loss	.82	Avg trade (win & loss)	$20.85
Max consec. Winners	9	Max consec. losers	3
Avg # bars in winners	8	Avg # bars in losers	12
Max intraday drawdown		($257.44)	
Profit Factor	2.03	Max # contracts held	99

TABLE 7-1: HISTORICAL PERFORMANCE OF THE P-INDICATOR FOR MSFT

TradeStation Strategy Performance Report - PIL INTC.HIS-Daily (1/2/96-1/31/00)

Performance Summary: All Trades

Total Net Profit	$1,484.24	Open position P/L	($4.40)
Gross Profit	$3,930.35	Gross Loss	($2,446.11)
Total # of trades	94	Percent profitable	64.89%
Number winning trades	61	Number losing trades	33
Largest winning trade	$98.28	Largest losing trade	($108.87)
Average winning trade	$64.43	Average losing trade	($74.12)
Ratio avg win/avg loss	.87	Avg trade (win & loss)	$15.79
Max consec. Winners	9	Max consec. losers	4
Avg # bars in winners	7	Avg # bars in losers	6
Max intraday drawdown		($377.46)	
Profit Factor	1.61	Max # contracts held	75

TABLE 7-2: HISTORICAL PERFORMANCE OF THE P-INDICATOR FOR INTC

SECTION THREE

TRADING METHODS AND SYSTEMS BASED ON PRICE PATTERNS

There are several misconceptions and fallacies surrounding the use of mechanical trading systems. One of the most predominant of these misconceptions is that the benefit in using a mechanical trading system comes from taking out the human emotion from the trading process. Of course, nothing can be farther from the truth! A mechanical trading system is just a tool, often comes in the form of computer software while the emotion of a trader is a psychological state. The two are not and should not be connected, unless one believes that the software becomes a part of the trader's thought process. Until such a technological breakthrough takes place, the mechanical trading system and the human using it will remain two separate entities. The fear of risking money that most traders experience and often prevents them from executing the trades that a mechanical trading system generates, will always be there, as long as the human is a part of the process. Blindly following a mechanical trading system, without being influenced by market developments and avoiding forming a personal opinion about future market direction that may be opposed to that of the system, is one of the most difficult tasks of a trader. But that has nothing to do with the trading system per se: it has more to do with the experience and discipline of the trader himself.

Another gross misconception is that everyone can develop a mechanical trading system using one of the popular software packages sold and designed for just this purpose. Undoubtedly, those packages offer a software platform that facilitates rapid trading system development and testing. However, developing anything significant requires a special mix of skills: knowledge of the markets and the trading process, mathematics, statistics and computer programming. Unless the right mix is present, the resulting trading systems often prove to be a failure. The concept of developing a winning trading system may sound, at least in theory, easy, but in practice it is one of the most difficult things to accomplish—almost like a license to print your own money!

The idea that one can buy a mechanical trading system from an ad in a magazine and become rich is just another fallacy! Profitable trading systems are not sold to the public because they simply make the kind of money that cannot be made by software sales alone. If someone has a good trading system, the only legitimate objective would be to use it and make money. Selling it to the public will just defy the main purpose for which the system was developed, *i.e.* to gain a competitive advantage over other traders. As soon as the system is in the open, the competitive advantage is lost. This, of course, does not include the case of custom trading system development services that some offer but just those systems that are intended for the mass market.

In this section of the book I first present the basic foundation needed for the development of mechanical trading systems based on price patterns. The trading methodologies I describe comprise a systematic trading framework that attempts to minimize the influence of factors outside the scope of the trading process, such as errors and human emotions. The latter part of this section deals with some advanced properties of trading systems based on price patterns and a basic discussion on money management.

Developing a winning trading system leads to a long path filled with unsuccessful attempts and frustration. Reward comes only to those that are devoted and are very persistent in their pursuit of this goal. The gains can be enormous but there is a steep learning curve to climb. Depending on previous experience and background, it may take longer for some than for others. But unless someone puts a personal effort into this there will be no achievement. Trading is a personal endeavor and the profits are yours to spend!

CHAPTER EIGHT

MANUAL TRADING TECHNIQUES

YOU DO NOT NEED A COMPUTER TO TRADE!

In the technological craze of our time, many have been led to believe that a mechanical trading system is a synonym to a complicated computer system that performs millions of mathematical operations a second driven by sophisticated algorithms and software. Many are also overwhelmed constantly reading in the papers the words "black-box trading" and "computer trading." These are just buzzwords! Usually, behind those seemingly very advanced trading systems are hidden very simple rules that account for a few basic algebraic manipulations. The main reason they are implemented in the computer is that in this way trading action can take place in a fast and efficient manner, avoiding any errors caused by human involvement under stressful conditions. This is necessary in the case of Institutional trading activity that deals with thousands or even hundreds of different issues on a daily basis. In many cases, the so-called "computer trading programs" just involve specific price levels where shares are either bought or sold to rebalance portfolios. Operators often input these price levels manually into these systems.

It is my opinion that the individual trader's community has grossly misused and abused the concept of a mechanical trading system. Most of the effort is put in developing complicated trading models that are a mix of mathematical formulas, technical analysis indicators and heuristics. Very little effort is spent to really understand the basic concepts behind modeling and how all these indicators and formulas can be used effectively to develop profitable trading systems. The usual routine is as follows: pick an indicator and test it historically. If it doesn't work throw it away or add another indicator and test gain. Then, if this does not work try another indicator.... And so on. Some of those developers if asked to describe the formula of the indicator used in their model will not even know it! This is really like "searching for a needle in a hay stack!" It leads nowhere.

Many successful traders do not use a computer to trade! Some do not even use a real-time quote screen! Those traders use very simple rules that have proved to work over time and can be monitored with the use of a sheet of paper and a pencil. One of the reasons they are successful is that they know very well what they are doing. They do it consistently and believe in it. They also prefer to do it manually because that gives them a "feel" of the market.

I am not advocating here this other extreme. Mechanical trading systems implemented in a computer are very useful if applied in the appropriate manner and backed by a solid understanding of their inner workings and operation. However, what I would suggest is that if a mechanical trading system involves such complex mathematical operations that absolutely requires a computer for its implementation then the chances of success are limited.

Computers have proved very useful in getting a fast and efficient historical testing of, even the simplest, trading systems. The need there is real and there is great value added. Furthermore, computer models designed to discover trading rules, such as the pattern search techniques of section two, can also be of great importance and value. However, the resulting trading rules must be simple and easy to understand. This is exactly the case with price patterns. Although the process of discovering them may be very involved and complicated, their logic, or trading rules, is very simple. That allows ease of monitoring and implementation, even in a manual mode.

A Manual Trading Method

Many successful traders use manual trading methods and feel very comfortable with them, as they have become a part of their daily routine. Some methods require more work than others. In cases where the value of an indicator must be calculated then a manual trading method involves extra effort. The price patterns presented in this book do not involve any complex mathematical operations. Their logic, or trading rules, consists of a number of simple conditions on the values of the parameters of the price bars that contribute to the pattern formation. In order to determine whether the trading rules are valid as of the close of a daily or intraday bar, one has to compare the magnitudes of a hand full of parameters. No addition, subtraction, division or multiplication! It is as simple as that! If the trading rules are valid, then the patterns are said to "have generated a signal" or a new trading position.

I will illustrate here a very simple, but yet powerful, manual trading technique that anyone with access to a daily newspaper can use to trade stocks short-term. No computers, Internet accesses or quote screens needed, just a pencil, a sheet of paper along with the will to be a winner.

To start, I recall the Gamma pattern logic presented in example 1 of chapter four:

$$C[2] > C[1] \text{ and } C[1] > C[0] \text{ and } C[0] > C[3]$$

A complete trading system based on the Gamma pattern is as follows:

If C[2] > C[1] and C[1] > C[0] and C[0] > C[3] then
Buy S number of shares tomorrow on the open with
profit target at entry price * (1 + T_p/100) and
stop-loss at entry price * (1 - T_s/100)

Where: S = C/entry price, C = trading capital allocated
and: T_p and T_s the percent profit target and
stop-loss, respectively.

The Gamma pattern may be used to trade several stocks. In the example, three of those stocks are considered, Microsoft (MSFT), Intel (INTC) and AT&T (T).

The *first step* in this manual trading method is to describe the pattern logic in simple English language as follows:

Close of 2 days ago greater than Close of yesterday and
Close of yesterday greater than Close of today and
Close of today greater than Close of 3 days ago

The next step is to identify the parameters present in the rules. In this case, those are:

Close of today
Close of Yesterday
Close of 2 days ago
Close of 3 days ago

The English-like rules can then be written on a sheet of paper, or worksheet, along with the details of the pattern, such as which stocks are traded and the profit targets and stops applicable in each case. The result, *step three,* may look like the worksheet shown in figure 8-1.

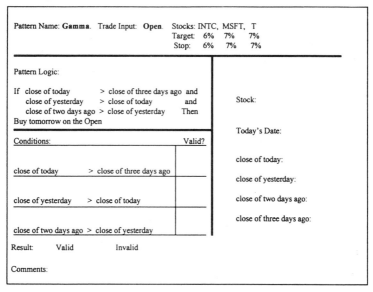

FIGURE 8-1: MANUAL TRADING WORKSHEET

On the top are listed the pattern name, the entry point, and the list of stocks along with the profit targets. Then the worksheet is split into two sections. The left lists the pattern logic and the English-like rules and the right the trading date, specific stock traded and parameters required to evaluate the pattern logic.

The next step, *four,* is to make enough copies of the worksheet, so it can be used in each trading day.

The *fifth step* involves the evaluation of the pattern rules by considering the actual values of the parameters involved as of the close of a particular trading day. This must be repeated separately for each stock traded by the Gamma pattern. Assuming that the last trading day is as of 07/27/99 and the traded stock is MSFT, the trader can fill in the appropriate values on the worksheet as shown in figure 8-2.

Pattern Name: **Gamma**. Trade Input: **Open**. Stocks: INTC, MSFT, T
Target: 6% 7% 7%
Stop: 6% 7% 7%

Pattern Logic:

If close of today   > close of three days ago   and
    close of yesterday   > close of today   and
       close of two days ago > close of yesterday   Then
Buy tomorrow on the Open

Stock: **INTC**

Conditions:		Valid?
67.5347 63.8487		YES
close of today > close of three days ago		
62.8491 67.5347		NO
close of yesterday > close of today		
64.1611 62.8491		YES
close of two days ago > close of yesterday		

Today's Date: 7/27/99

close of today: 67.5347

close of yesterday: 62.8491

close of two days ago: 64.1611

close of three days ago: 63.8487

Result: Valid   Invalid   V

Comments:

FIGURE 8-2: COMPLETING THE WORKSHEET

The conditions are then evaluated by just comparing the values on top of them. The result is noted next to the condition — Yes if valid and No if invalid. All conditions must be valid in order for the pattern to generate a signal. In the example of figure 8-2, two conditions are valid and one is invalid. Therefore, there in no signal generated. This is noted in the result line below the conditions.

The five steps involved in this simple manual trading method must be repeated for each stock listed in the worksheet. This is essentially a manual signal tracking of a trading system. It is also evident that as the number of patterns and followed stocks increases, the efficiency of such a method decreases. Nevertheless, for a trader that follows just a few stocks it can prove to be very helpful. It may also prove to be a good exercise before one starts developing more advanced mechanical trading systems methods.

I will emphasize here that the manual trading method described in this chapter is more suitable to short-term trading and patterns formed by daily bars. Trading using intraday patterns cannot be easily accomplished with such a manual method, simply because there may not be enough time to evaluate the patterns logic. In that case, the need for an automatic method is real.

CHAPTER NINE

TRADING SYSTEM MODELING

The recent technological progress in personal computer hardware and software has transferred a lot of computing power to the hands of individual traders, at a very low cost. This is almost equivalent to the same processing power and analysis capabilities that only an institutional trader possessed in the past.

The real breakthrough came in the late 80's when the first software products designed to provide a platform for trading system modeling and back-testing appear on the open market. The developers of these software packages claimed then that anyone with basic computer skills could use those software packages to develop, or even discover, trading systems and profit. Undoubtedly, those software packages provided many advantages to the trading system developer, such as speed of implementation and testing. When the fad went away, however, a few facts became clear: first, those packages were not so easy to use and programming anything above average required good programming skills. Second, these programs had hidden assumptions about trading and some operational limitations that were a serious impediment to their use under many circumstances. Third and maybe most important, what is true about computational software in general, holds also true in that case: garbage in — garbage out!

121

There can be no dispute that the most important step in the development of a trading system is coming up with a idea, or a model, that works, that is, it generates trades with a high enough profitability rate. In order to achieve this, one must develop a specific theoretical framework of market operation. Then, the theory must be translated into a language that allows a quantitative assessment, *i.e.* Mathematics. This process is called *modeling*. The result of it is called the *model*. This process is the same in every field that deals with any short of predictions or forecasts, such as in Economics, Meteorology and Queuing Theory, to name a few. Without a theoretical framework, the task of discovering a profitable trading system model may be a hopeless one. Most trading system developers will never achieve their goal, since their approach is based on the trial-and-error method of back-testing using indicators and formulas that do not fit into any specific theoretical framework.

In section one of this book, I presented a basic framework on using patterns to trade stocks. This framework is essentially the modeling process. The pattern search methods of section two were based on that framework and were a direct outcome, or implementation, of the modeling process. The actual patterns found by the search methods are the models that are used to develop short-term trading systems.

The stock market is a real world system formed by all its participants, called here "the traders." As shown in figure 9-1, the input to this system is made up of news, information about the market and other markets and future expectations about price levels. The output of the system, at every particular instance, is the price of a security and has three possible levels: up, down or steady. That is true for any time frame considered, such as a minute, five minutes, daily, weekly or even monthly.

The objective of a trading system developer is to find a model that will approximate the real system behavior to a satisfactory extend. However, although the output states of the system in figure 9-1 are only three, the process that generates them is highly non-linear and stochastic. In every instance in time, the output of the system is the resultant action taken by each of the market participants, called here the traders. Any knowledge of the past levels of the output stated is of no use in the forecasting of future levels since neither the market participants nor the individual processes that drive their decisions are known. Approaching the modeling process from this angle always proves to be a hopeless task.

The "practical" approach to the market modeling problem is to construct a mathematical model that will approximate the real market behavior in the sense that the model output will coincide with the market output on certain instances called the "Entry Points" or "Entry Signals." Every entry signal will have a corresponding "Exit Point" or "Exit Signal." At these specific instances, the developer makes the assumption that the non-linear and stochastic effects are minimized and a much simpler model can be a satisfactory approximation of the real system. The input to the model is the price history of the market and its length depends on the number of bars that the model uses to "look" in the past in order to forecast the future, as shown in Figure 9-2. E and X stand for the generated market entry and exit points.

This type of modeling approach makes many assumptions and can only result in models that have limited predicting power. While in other application areas the results would only be seen as carrying a forecasting error, trading models have an additional shortcoming: they generate money losses. The objective of the developer is then to limit these losses as much as possible. This is accomplished in practice if the sum of all losses, or losing trades, that the model generates is smaller than the sum of all gains, or profitable trades, over a sufficiently longer period of time in the future. That is, the actual profitability of the model can never been known in advance. It can only be measured under real trading conditions by putting the model to work.

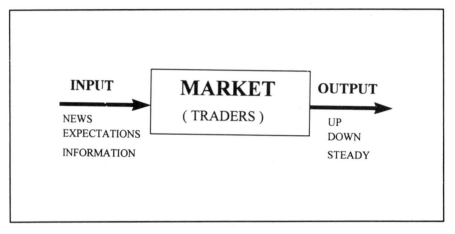

FIGURE 9-1: THE MARKET SYSTEM

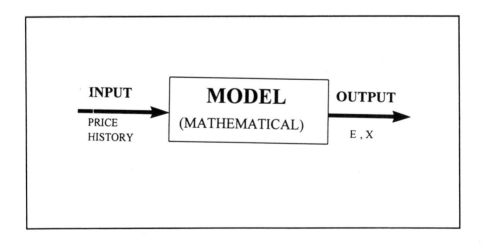

FIGURE 9-2: THE MARKET MODEL

Chapter Ten

Trading System Back-Testing

Back testing is the process of determining how a trading system model developed would have performed if it were being used to trade in the past. When a model of a trading system is available, the object of back testing is to use historical prices of a security and obtain a set of entry and exit points, as shown in Figure 10-1. The entry and exit points, shown as E_i and X_i, respectively, are then used in conjunction with the historical data input to calculate a set of very useful parameters. The process of back testing a trading system model with input made of actual historical data is also called "Historical Simulation" or "Historical Testing."

The usefulness of back testing comes from the arbitrary assumption, or hope, that a trading system model will behave in the future in a similar way as it has done in the past. The validity of such assumption cannot be tested before hand, but only by using the trading system model in actual trading in the future. Some developers attempt to increase the validity of this assumption and the significance of the results by developing and back testing a model using part of the historical data available and then forward-testing it for the remainder of the historical data. Adjustment of any parameters in the model takes place only in the back-testing portion of the process while they are kept constant in the forward-testing portion. This is still, however, a historical testing all together, and the problem of future performance is still valid and must be proven under real use. Nevertheless, in the absence of anything else, back testing is the only way of knowing how a model behaved in the past. Regardless, of how it will behave in the future, most traders would prefer to use a model that performed well in the past, as opposed to one that did not. However, I have to make a note here that this is not backed by rigorous analysis and it is just an empirical practice.

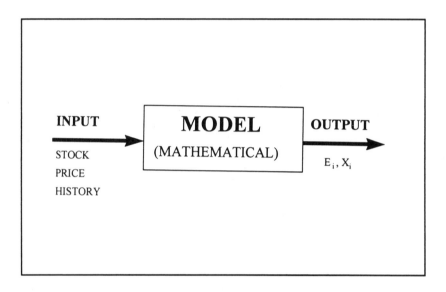

FIGURE 10-1: THE PROCESS OF BACK-TESTING

The back-testing process assumes that a sufficient length of historical data is used. This is a serious shortcoming in the case of a security that does not have enough trading history, such as a new issue. There are a couple of choices that can be tried in such cases: a) a similar security may be used that has sufficient data history or, b) a data history can be made up using an appropriate historical data generator. Both of these options do not guarantee the same type of reliability of the results obtained.

Probably, the most serious assumption, and maybe the least talked about, is that the trading system model tested and the data that it is tested on are two independent processes. This is *great fallacy* because when a trading model is actually used to trade it affects prices, simply because it is one of the factors that affect demand and supply in the market. When a model is back-tested, such affect is not taken directly into account. There are several ways to minimize such an affect, the most important being to trade very liquid markets where there is always enough demand to absorb all supply, and *vice versa*. Another, more technical way, is to have a trading system model that generates a sufficiently high number of trades where the statistical law of large numbers can be affective. In such case, any unfavorable affects in prices will tend to be counteracted by other favorable affects in the longer term. However, this assumes that the affect of the trading model is of "local" nature and does not cause major changes, such as trend reversals. In that case, the use of back-testing is not valid. Most popular stock issues and futures markets are "deep" enough so that no single player can affect market direction in the longer term. Care should be exercised when back testing using intraday data. Under certain circumstances, such as very small profit targets and stops, the results can be very misleading. I would recommend extra care when using back testing for trading system models that intend to "scalp" markets, for this reason.

THE BACK-TESTING PROCESS

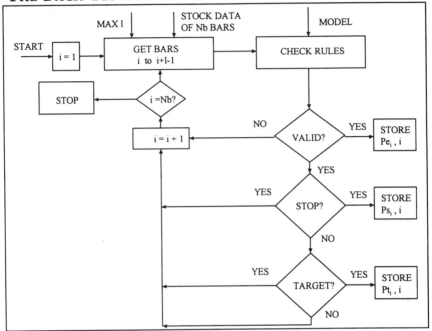

FIGURE 10-2: BACK-TESTING PROCESS BLOCK DIAGRAM

Figure 10-2 shows a block diagram of the back-testing process. It starts by considering a trading system model and a historical data file that contains Nb records. In the case of daily data, each record represents a trading day and, usually, has the following form:

Date, Open, High, Low, Close, Volume

In the case of intraday data, the historical file records may look as follows:

Date, Time, Open, High, Low, Close, Volume

The first date in the data file is usually the oldest record and the last, the most recent. The testing starts by considering the first l bars, a number equal to the maximum bar sequence length that can be found in the model. The model rules are then checked to determine if they are all satisfied. If any of the rules are not satisfied, then the testing continues by adding the next bar in the data file to the first l bars and dropping the last one. Alternatively, if all the rules are satisfied that implies there is a position to be established, long or short depending on the particular model. When the position is established, the entry price Pe_i is recorded along with its index, i, which denote the bar count. The testing then goes on by checking whether the stop-loss is hit first. In order to accomplish this, the price where the stop is to be executed, Ps_i, is determined according to the stop-loss specified in the model. Then, the historical data is used, starting from the entry point, in order to determine whether the stop is hit. The data count is increments by one (not shown on Figure 10-2) and the following test is made:

For long positions:

If Low < Ps_i Then Stop

For short positions:

If High > Ps_i Then Stop

If the stop is not hit, then a test is performed to determine whether the profit target is hit. For this purpose, first the price, Pt_i, at which the trade will be exited with profit, is determined according to the profit target specified in the model:

For long positions:

129

If High > Pt$_i$ Then Target

For short positions:

If Low < Pt$_i$ Then Target

If the target is not hit either, then the next bar is tested, and so on, until a stop or profit target is hit. In the case that either the stop-loss or the profit target is hit, the appropriate price is stored along with the trade count. The file created then, among other information, may contain the following:

Bar Count, Entry price or Exit price (Stop Price or Profit Price)

The testing is repeated until the last bar, Nb, in the historical data file is considered. It may be possible that there will not be enough data in the file to determine whether the last trade exited with a profit or loss, when such a trade originated near the file end. In such a case, that is considered as an open position when the last close in the file is used to calculate whether there is an open trade profit or loss.

Testing for a stop before a profit is the worst case scenario that always produces conservative results. This is also the assumption made in most of the back-testing software programs that are sold in the marketplace, in the form of pre-packaged software. In the case of daily bars, for instance, there is no way to know whether the low of the day or the high of the day was actually formed first, and therefore the worst case is considered. An improved back-testing algorithm should involve the simultaneous consideration of tick-by-tick data to determine conditions "inside a bar," both for daily and intraday historical data. However, this makes back testing a slow and expensive procedure. (Tick data are expensive to buy.)

BACK-TESTING IMPLEMENTATION

The back-testing process just described can be implemented in the computer using any high level programming language. Alternatively, any of the commercial software packages sold for this purpose may be used. The advantages in using those popular software packages are many as compared to writing code. These packages offer an integrated platform for trading system modeling and back-testing, in a user friendly environment that provides everything, from technical analysis formulas and indicators to historical data bases and analysis of the results. The disadvantage is that these software programs are black-boxes and their "ease" of use comes at the expense of the knowledge of their inner workings and any assumptions made. The learning curve in being able to use successfully and productively such software packages may get considerably long. Therefore, a trading system developer should carefully make a decision whether the time spent in learning how to use these packages will be of benefit in his or her particular case. It is my opinion that development of anything beyond average that provides a competitive advantage, such as the pattern search algorithms described in section two of this book, requires writing custom code. This presents a problem to traders that do not have experience with programming—and not everyone should. However, there are a few solutions there including hiring a programmer either on an hourly basis or on a profit share basis. The cost will be more than justified in the longer term.

ANALYSIS OF THE BACK-TESTING RESULTS

The file generated by the back testing process, listing all entry and exit prices along with the bar count, or date (and time if intraday) of occurrence can be used to analyze the historical performance of a trading system model. The parameters of importance were discussed in the performance analysis section of chapter four of this book. The definitions are the same, regardless of whether the trading system model includes one or many patterns.

Correct interpretation of the results obtained by the back-testing process can only be made in the context of the model intended operation. This is a subjective analysis, as there is no absolute measure to compare it to. Therefore, the trading system developer should always keep the modeling goals and objectives in perspective and not be allured by results that are seemingly good but are not justified by the model intended operation. Good back-testing results do not always imply a good trading system.

CHAPTER ELEVEN

PUTTING PATTERNS TO WORK

Patterns can be combined to form trading system models and used in short-term or day trading. This can be done irrespectively of the method used to identify the individual patterns from historical chart data. An automatic search method greatly speeds up the process of generating a sufficiently large number of patterns needed to put together a trading system model.

A Pattern Combination Model, (PCM), exhibits very interesting properties that can greatly enhance the ability of a trader to profit by allowing various risk and money management alternatives. The opportunities present will be discussed further in chapter 12. The subject of this chapter is to illustrate the procedure of constructing a PCM and its use in generating trading signals in a systematic way.

DEVELOPING A PATTERN COMBINATION MODEL (PCM)

Figure 11-1 shows the development procedure followed in combining patterns together to form a mechanical trading system model. A description of each step follows:

133

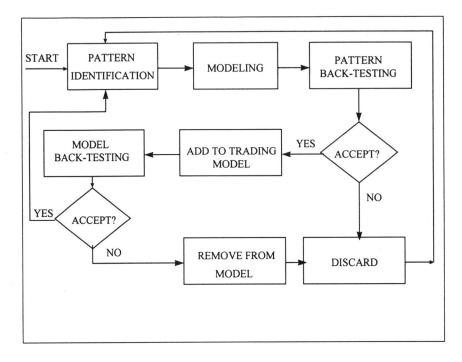

FIGURE 11-1: DEVELOPING A PCM

PATTERN IDENTIFICATION:

The pattern identification may be based on any of the methods discussed in section two of this book. It can either be a manual method, such as the visual search technique, or an automatic method such as the Combinatorial Pattern Formation (CPF) or the Exhaustive Pattern Search (EPS) method.

PATTERN BACK-TESTING:

The back-testing step is usually an integral part of an automatic pattern search method, or can be performed separately, in the case of a manual pattern search. The objective of this step is to determine whether a selected pattern is acceptable, in the form of a stand-alone trading model. The criteria for making such a decision was discussed in chapter 4. If the historical performance based on these criteria is not satisfactory, then the pattern is discarded.

ADD TO TRADING MODEL:

The trading model slowly grows by adding patterns that satisfy the performance criteria established in advance. Each new addition is made by supplementing the trading model rules to account for the new pattern. This can be done in several ways. One way is to combine, or group, patterns based on the profit target and stops-loss used. That is, the logic of patterns that have the same profit target and stop-loss can be combined into a single-trading rule. Another choice is to treat each distinct pattern as a separate sub-model of the combined model. The ultimate choice may depend on various other considerations, such as, for instance, whether trading signals that are generated by patterns in the same direction as an already open position initiated by another pattern are allowed. There is a lot of flexibility in this process and, as a consequence, many possibilities arise. Some of these possibilities are discussed in the next chapter.

MODEL BACK-TESTING:

Each new pattern added to the trading model alters its performance characteristics, simply because it contributes to additional signal generation. For this reason the new trading model must be back-tested, each time a new addition is made. The purpose for doing this is twofold: first to check for any possible errors in the addition of the new pattern rules, especially in the case that this is done in a manual way. Second, to investigate the possibility of any adverse interaction of the new pattern with the already selected patterns. This includes the case where the new pattern is completely redundant, *i.e.* its addition to the model does not contribute to any new trades or to the improvement of the performance.

The *Pattern Interaction Ratio*, R_{pl}, is defined as the total number of historical trades of a PCM divided by the sum of the historical trades generated individually by each pattern when back-tested separately. A recommended figure for that ratio is 0.5 or higher. A ratio of 0.7 or above is highly desirable, if possible.

Let a PCM formed by k different patterns. Also, let N_t be the number of trades generated by the PCM when back-tested over a sufficiently long historical period and N_{tk} the trades generated by each of the k patterns when back-tested over the same time period. Then:

$$R_{pl} = \frac{N_t}{\sum\limits_{i=1}^{k} N_{ti}}$$

If any further addition of a pattern causes this ratio to drop below a preset level, such as the suggested 0.50, then the pattern may be removed from the model and discarded. This, however, is one mathematical measure and there may be other considerations for keeping a pattern in the model. Such special considerations may include parameters such as the pattern type and sequence length. If the alleged redundant pattern has a long bar sequence then it may be a good idea to retain it.

The process of combining patterns to form a PCM may, at least theoretically, go on forever. In practice, the process stops when any new addition of patterns does not contribute any longer to the performance of the model, to the increase of trades generated by back-testing, or there is a consistent degradation in pattern interaction, as measured by the ratio R_{pI} .

USING A TRADING MODEL

Many traders think that the development of a profitable system is all that is needed to succeed. In reality, this is the point where the real hard work starts! The objective is using the trading model in a systematic way and executing the trading signals generated with discipline. The influence of factors alien to the decision process of the model must be minimized or even neutralized completely. That will allow the maximum benefit that a mechanical trading system can offer, which is eliminating emotion and irrational actions from the trading process.

Trading models constructed by combining patterns, called here PCM's, require some additional effort in real life use. These trading models may involve dozens or even hundreds of patterns with different entry points and profit target and stop-loss levels. In addition, the patterns may be grouped in different classes, some allowing interaction of trading signals and some not. This flexibility provides increased opportunity but also presents a logistical problem. This can be handled in an efficient way by an operational framework. The benefit of this framework is not limited to the correct application of the trading model. It further provides a systematic approach to trading the markets that induces discipline and keeps the trader focused on the objectives at hand.

The process that I describe next is about developing a daily trading plan. In short, the plan allows determining the position status of the patterns in a trading model, establishing profit targets and stops and determining in advance potential market entry points.

The block diagram of the operation if shown in figure 11-2.

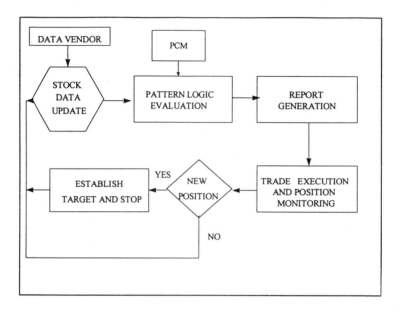

FIGURE 11-2: USING A TRADING MODEL

PATTERN LOGIC EVALUATION:

Each pattern in the pattern combination model is considered separately and its logic evaluated to determine whether there is a new trading signal. When there is a large number of patterns, this should be done in a mechanized fashion. Custom code may be developed for this purpose. Some popular trading packages offer this function and can be used effectively for this purpose. For a reasonably low number of patterns, the manual procedure described in chapter eight may be used.

Report Generation:

The report compiles all information useful in the daily trading activity. It is a trading plan that lists all open positions, profit target levels and stops, and any new positions to be placed. Usually, only those patterns that have an open position or have generated a new position are listed. The remaining patterns, with a "flat" position are not included in the report.

Some of the patterns in a trading model generate entry signals at the open of the next day or at a specific price level of the next day but some may also do that at the close of the day that the pattern formation is completed. For this latter type of patterns it is useful to determine a day in advance the conditions that will make them valid, *i.e.* generate a trading signal. Since the only unknowns are the open, high, low and close of the next day, the appropriate conditions can be determined in accordance to the logic of each pattern and the range of values that will guarantee validation. I call this the "Next Day Projection" technique NDP. A more detailed description of this technique will be given later in this chapter.

Trade Execution and Position Monitoring:

Any new positions listed on the trading plan for the open of the next day are executed as soon as the market opens. If the trading model includes patterns that generate positions at the close of the last bar in their formation then during the course of the trading day, the trader must monitor stock prices and check all the various conditions listed in the trading report. Any conditions listed that are not valid any longer due to new price levels developing are crossed out along with the specific pattern. As the trading day comes to an end, most conditions are usually invalidated and there are a small number of patterns with a possibility to generate a signal at the close.

139

If validation of the conditions of a pattern near the close is not possible due to price fluctuation or such validation cannot be made with certainty then the trader must wait for the market close without executing a position. The conditions can then be evaluated and if there is a signal generated the corresponding position can be entered either at the beginning of any after-hours session, if that is applicable, or at the open of the next trading day. That may cause some slippage, but in the longer term these occasional variations usually average out to zero.

In the case that the trading system model has an open position in a particular stock, long or short, and another trading signal is generated in the same direction this new signal is usually neglected. However, this signal may be viewed as a confirmation of the open position and used to move the original position stops to a new price level, as if the new trading signal is in affect. There are many ways to treat multiple trading signals, a unique property of pattern combination models. A discussion that deals with this subject is given in the next chapter.

ESTABLISH PROFIT AND STOP:

Each time a new position is initiated, the profit target and stop-loss must be noted from the report and either placed as an open order or kept as a "mental" stop. Some traders are hesitant in placing, especially stop orders, as open orders. This fear originates from the common view that market makers "run stops." This may be true and, actually part of how markets work towards balancing demand and supply. If the stop price is sufficiently far away and the market traded liquid enough then there is very little room for price manipulation by market makers, as they are busy providing liquidity and making a good profit from the bid-ask spreads. For instance, a Microsoft long position at $100 per-share with a 6% stop-loss results in a stop price per share of $94, which is a good distance away for the market maker to chase. In the case of day trading, however, profit target and stop-loss levels are significantly smaller and that may present problems more often. Definitely avoid placing stops in this case, irrespectively of market liquidity. Market makers will definitively "run" them down! It is just how markets work.

EXAMPLE OF A TRADING REPORT

A typical example of a report generated by the trading process of figure 11-2 is shown in figure 11-3. On its top is listed the date of the report generation, which also refers to the market close of that specific trading day, and the name of the trading system model in use. The report is then divided into two sections: one for long trading signals and the other for short. Each section is identical and sub-divided further into three more sections: The first section lists all the patterns that have generated new positions that must be placed as of the open of the next trading day. The second lists all the patterns that are in an open position and the third lists patterns that generate signals for the close of the day and the corresponding conditions that will make them valid. Next to the conditions, the corresponding profit target and stop-loss are also indicated.

Please note that this type of report deals only with signal tracking and does not involve any portfolio management features. As a consequence of this, the number of shares that must be bought or sold short is not indicated on this particular report but it is left to be the task of additional processing that must be done after the report is generated.

FIGURE 11-3: TRADING REPORT EXAMPLE

TRADING REPORT   DATE: 10/01/1999

LONG PATTERNS

NEW ENTRIES - TRADE INPUT AT OPEN OF TOMORROW

PATTERN CODE	STOCK		TARGET	STOP
0024	INTC		6%	6%
0035	GE		5%	5%

OPEN POSITIONS

PATTERN CODE	STOCK	DATE	TARGET	STOP
0072	CSCO	09/30/1999	6%	6%

CONDITIONS FOR NEW POSITION AT THE CLOSE OF TOMORROW

PATTERN CODE	STOCK	CONDITIONS
0057	MSFT	H > 93.625 - L > 91.25 - C > 93.125 - 5% - 5%

SHORT PATTERNS

NEW ENTRIES - TRADE INPUT AT OPEN OF TOMORROW

PATTERN CODE	STOCK		TARGET	STOP
NO ENTRIES				

OPEN POSITIONS

PATTERN CODE	STOCK	DATE	TARGET	STOP
NO ENTRIES				

CONDITIONS FOR NEW POSITION AT THE CLOSE OF TOMORROW

PATTERN CODE	STOCK	CONDITIONS
0145	INTC	H < 77.9375 - C < 72.625 - 6% - 6%

THE NEXT DAY PROJECTION (NDP) TECHNIQUE

Patterns that generate positions that must be placed at the close of the day that their formation is complete require some additional work in order to be able to use them efficiently. The "Next Day Projection Technique," (NDP), allows determining which patterns qualify to generate a position at the close of the next day and the corresponding conditions that must be met, according to each pattern's logic. In essence, this technique is based on filtering out those patterns for which a definite conclusion can be made that they cannot generate a trading signal at the close of the next day, irrespectively of that day's trading range, and keeping those whose final validation is pending on the next day's price trading range.

In order to illustrate this technique with a practical example, let us consider a pattern with the following logic:

If $H[1] > L[1]$ and $H[2] > H[1]$ and $H[1] > L[0]$ and $L[1] > L[2]$ and $L[0] > L[1]$ and $C[0] > H[2]$ then buy today on the close.

Where the index 0 denotes the last trading day, or today, 1 is yesterday and 2 is the day before yesterday. The pattern is shown in figure 11-4 and corresponds to an inside day formation, as shown by the first two bars, labeled 2 and 1, followed by a breakout of the close of the last bar, 0, above the high of bar 2.

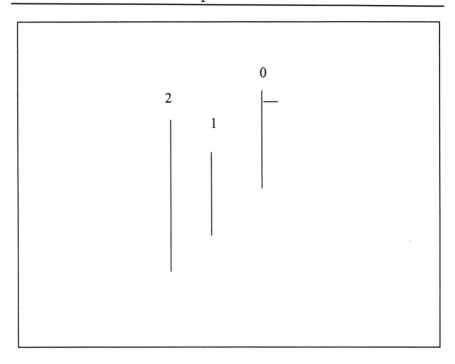

FIGURE 11-4: INSIDE BAR BREAK-OUT PATTERN EXAMPLE

The first step in the NDP technique is to list all the individual conditions separately, as shown below:

1 H[1] > L[1]
2. H[2] > H[1]
3. L[1] > L[2]
4. L[0] > L[1]
5. C[0] > H[2]

There are five different conditions involved in the pattern logic. The next step is to make a forward shift of the indexes. This is accomplished by reducing each index by one. The shift results in the following conditions:

1. H[0] > L[0]
2. H[1] > H[0]
3. L[0] > L[1]
4. L[-1] > L[0]
5. C[-1] > H[1]

Due to the shift, today becomes tomorrow, yesterday becomes today and the day before yesterday becomes yesterday, as illustrated in figure 11-5. The negative index, -1, can be omitted for clarity and the projected rules are then as follows:

1. H[0] > L[0]
2. H[1] > H[0]
3. L[0] > L[1]
4. L   > L[0]
5. C   > H[1]

Any quantities that have a negative index, which is omitted for clarity, are called "no-index" quantities. As of the close of a specific day, all of the C[0], L[0], H[1] and L[1] have a specific numeric value. All the conditions that do not involve any no-index quantities are those that must be valid as of the close of the last trading day in order for that pattern to be a candidate for signal generation. Then, for final pattern validation, the next day price range must satisfy all conditions that involve a quantity with a no-index. In the example above, after the shift in indexes, the following conditions do not involve any no-indexes:

1. H[0] > L[0]
2. H[1] > H[0]
3. L[0] > L[1]

and must be valid in order to proceed further. If valid, then the attention is turned to those conditions that involve no-indexes, which must be valid on the following day. In this particular case,

there are two conditions to be met:
4. L > L[0]
5. C > H[1]

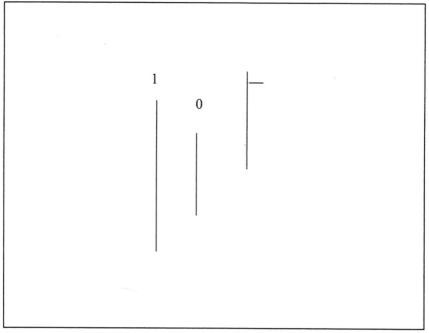

*FIGURE 11-5: BAR SHIFT USING THE **NDP** TECHNIQUE*

If a bar chart formation of an inside bar has formed then, as of the close of a particular day, the conditions for the pattern to generate a signal are that the low of the next day be higher than the low of today and the close of the next day be higher than the high of yesterday.

If at any moment during the course of the next trading day the low falls below the value L[0] then the pattern seizes to be a candidate for generating a position because one of its conditions has been permanently invalidated.

A GENERAL APPROACH TO NDP:

Let us consider a price pattern that is formed by l consecutive chart bars and has k conditions for generating a trading signal at the close of the lst bar. The k conditions involve only the open, high, low and close of any of the l bars. A general procedure is as follows:

Step 1: Label all bars starting from 0, for the last, up to l - 1

Step 2: The open, high, low and close for the j bar are denoted as follows, in all k conditions:

$$\text{open} = O[j]$$
$$\text{high} = H[j]$$
$$\text{low} = L[j]$$
$$\text{close} = C[j] \quad , \quad \text{for all } j = 0,1,2,\ldots,l\text{-}1$$

Step 3: Subtract 1 from all the indexes found in all k conditions. That results as follows:

$$O[j] \rightarrow O[j\text{-}1]$$
$$H[j] \rightarrow H[j\text{-}1]$$
$$L[j] \rightarrow L[j\text{-}1]$$
$$C[j] \rightarrow C[j\text{-}1] \text{ , for all } j = 0,1,2,\ldots,l\text{-}1$$

The index "-1" is called a "no-index" and is denoted as follows:

$$O[\text{-}1] = O$$
$$H[\text{-}1] = H$$
$$L[\text{-}1] = L$$
$$C[\text{-}1] = C$$

Step 4: After the index shift, there are again k conditions that are separated into two categories:
a) conditions that do not contain O,H,L,C, *i.e.* do not involve any no-index quantities and
b) conditions that contain any of the O,H,L,C, *i.e.* involve no-index quantities.

Step 5: Check if all of the conditions that do not involve any no- indexes are true. If any not true then quit. If all true then continue.

Step 6: Solve for the ranges of O,H,L,C that will make all conditions that contain them valid.

The last step requires the simultaneous solution of a set of conditions. In their simplest form, as in our example above, these conditions are simple linear inequalities that involve only the variables O,H,L and C. The solution in this case is simple and any software program that may be required to automate the procedure can be developed fairly easy. More complicated conditions may require mathematical manipulations to be made. There are several ways to handle complex conditions, including manual solutions or the use of symbolic mathematics manipulation packages. When a Pattern Combination Model (PCM) is used and is made up of a large number of price patterns then a method to automatically solve the conditions of step 6 is necessary in order to provide the information required for the trading report generation.

CHAPTER TWELVE

ADVANCED PATTERNS TRADING

Trading system models using price patterns generate trading signals in numbers proportional to the number of patterns involved. The more patterns present, the more trading signals are available to the trader. In principle, one may distinguish at least three different types of trading signals, according to their timing of occurrence:

1. Signals indicating a position in the opposite direction of an already open position.
2. Signals indicating a position in the same direction of an already open position.
3. Signals that occur at exactly the same time all indicating a position in the same direction.

The first type of signals, as in 1 above, can be handled easily by just closing the open position. A riskier approach is to reverse position, by closing the open position and initiating a new one in the opposite direction. Experience has shown that occurrence of these type of signals is scarce.

Cases, 2 and 3 above, give rise to some very interesting properties of pattern based trading system models and provide advanced ways of managing the size of a position and its dollar risk. For this purpose, the following definitions are made.

Successive are called trading signals that generate a new position that is closed flat, by either hitting a profit target or a stop-loss, before the next signal arrives. The time period between successive trading signals is usually short, in the order of a few bars.

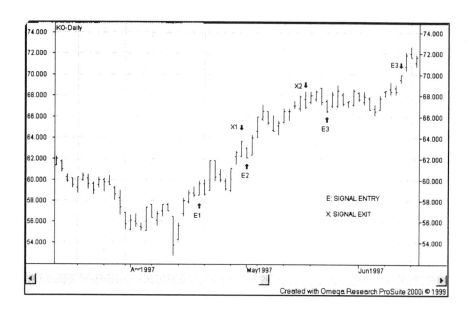

Created with Omega Research ProSuite 2000i © 1999

FIGURE 12-1: SUCCESSIVE TRADING SIGNALS

The concept of successive trading signals is illustrated in figure 12-1, a daily chart of Coca-Cola Co. (KO). Three successive trading signals are shown. The first signal initiates a position as "E1" and exits that position as "X1." The second trading signal follows one bar after the first has exited its position and it is labeled "E2" with its exit shown as "X2." The third signal is generated four bars after the second signal has exited, called "E3" and "X3."

Coincident is called trading signals with overlapping open positions. That is, one signal indicates a new position while another has an open position already in place. The trading signal direction must be the same; *i.e.* a long signal is generated while a long position is in place. Generation of the second signal must take place at least one bar after the first signal has generated its position.

Figure 12-2 shows an example of three coincident trading signals. The first signal is labeled "E1" and is in an open position while the second signal labeled "E4" is generated. The third signal, "E5" comes after the second signal. The last signal just happens to exit first, shown as "X5," followed by the first, shown as "X1" and the second, "X4."

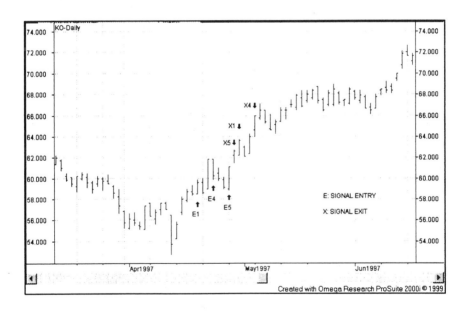

FIGURE 12-2: COINCIDENT TRADING SIGNALS

Clustered are called trading signals that generate new positions simultaneously, all in the same direction. Each clustered trading signal may have a different profit targets and stops loss level, as dictated by its pattern logic.

Figure 12-3 demonstrates an example of clustered trading signals. Signals seven and eight, labeled as "E7" and "E8" occur at the same time, although they exit at different points on the chart, labeled "X7" and "X8."

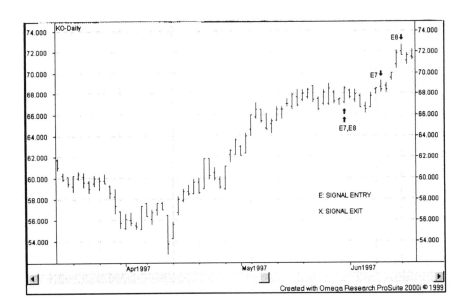

FIGURE 12-3: CLUSTERED TRADING SIGNALS

Figure 12-4 has been constructed by overlaying figures 12-1 through 12-3. All eight trading signals are shown. The following observations can be made on the resulting interaction, in accordance with the definitions given above:

Signals 1, 2 and 3 are consecutive.
Signals 1, 4 and 5 are coincident.
Signals 4, 5 and 2 are coincident.
Signals 3, 7 and 8 are coincident.
Signals 7 and 8 are clustered.

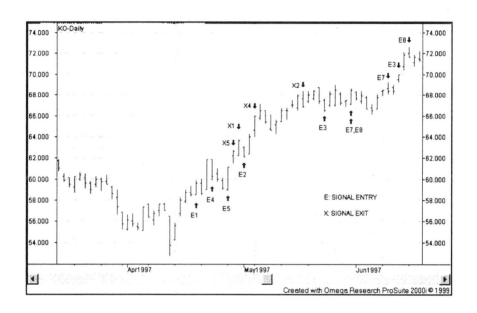

FIGURE 12-4: EXAMPLE OF A TRADING SIGNAL MIX

There are several ways that one can use the trading signals shown in figure 12-4. Some possibilities are given below:

a) *Ignoring coincident and clustered trading signals.* This is the simplest way of using trading system models based on price patterns. Whenever a signal is generated in the same direction with an already open position, that signal is just neglected. In the example of figure 12-4, only signals 1, 2 and 3 would have been taken into account.

b) *Using coincident signals to increase a position size.* When a coincident signal is generated, an already open position may be increased by a certain amount of shares. For instance, if there is an open long position of 400 shares resulting from signal 1 and signal 4 arrives, then 100 additional shares may be bought. The appropriate amount of shares must be estimated based on the risk parameters of the trading system model involved and it is not a simple task. It is recommended keeping the increase at a level equal to a fraction of the original position and to definitely avoid doubling of positions. Fractions of 10% to 30% seem to be on the safe side. The resulting position of 500 shares in total may be sold in full when exit 1 arrives in figure 12-4, an action that poses the lowest risk. Alternatively, each lot bought separately may be sold when the corresponding exit signal arrives, which represents a medium risk. The highest risk is assumed when one waits to unload the position at the exit of signal 4. Since this is further out in time, the probability of a market reversal may also be higher. The recommendation made here is to close positions at the first exit signals, E1, shown in figure 12-4.

c) *Using coincident signals for moving stops/targets.* This is one of the most useful applications of coincident signals. When a coincident signal arrives, it may be used to move an already placed stop-loss to a new level, in accordance with the requirements of the new signal. In our example shown in figure 12-4, when signal 4 arrives, there is a long position already open, generated by signal 1. The trader can just move the stop-loss associated with signal 1 to a new position corresponding to signal 4. This can be repeated again when signal

5 arrives. Conversely, the profit target may also be moved to a new level that corresponds to the profit target of the new signal. Moving the stop-loss has a similar effect with a trailing-stop, which is used in trend-following systems. In essence, if enough coincident trading signals are generated, the result is a trend-following action. This is, however, not a property of pattern based trading system models by design but a random event that is not under the control of the trader. If there is a great number of patterns in the trading system model, the chances of trend following become higher.

There are three possibilities as listed below:

<u>Moving the stop-loss and keeping the profit target fixed;</u> this is the lowest risk strategy with objective to minimize losses.

<u>Moving the stop-loss and the profit target;</u> this is a medium risk strategy resulting in reduced risk with increased profit potential.

<u>Keeping the stop-loss fixed and moving the profit target;</u> this is a high-risk strategy with the objective of maximizing profit while increasing the risk. It may also result in higher draw-downs.

d) *Use of clustered signals for signal confirmation.* When clusters of trading signals are generated, they can be interpreted as either a confirmation to any existing position or as a new position with increased probability of success. In the example in figure 12-4, the arrival of the cluster 7 and 8 right after signal 3 can serve as a confirmation. The trader may decide to increase the position size by buying additional shares. Since in this particular example the cluster coincides with signal 3, the profit target and/or stop-loss can be moved to a new level, offering increased flexibility for managing position size and risk.

TREND FOLLOWING WITH PRICE PATTERNS

Figure 12-5 shows a daily chart for General Electric Corporation for the period between August to December 1999. During this period the stock has risen from about $105 per share to about $160 per share, a sizable move of $55 per share. The three entry and exit signals shown on the chart are generated in a consecutive fashion by a pattern called GAP-2H. Details on the logic and performance of this pattern are given in the section 4 of this book. What is important to notice here is that the three consecutive trading signals generated just by a single pattern, managed to capture a sizable portion of the $55 move. Specifically, the back-testing analysis for this pattern shown in figure 12-6 indicates a total net profit of $26.44 for a unit share bought at every entry point, which corresponds to approximately 50% of the trend size during the tested period. The profit target and stop-loss were both equal to 7% for this test. This simple example indicates the potential of patterns generating successive trading signals and following a price trend. As the number of patterns is increased, so are the chances of increasing the portion of the trend that is captured.

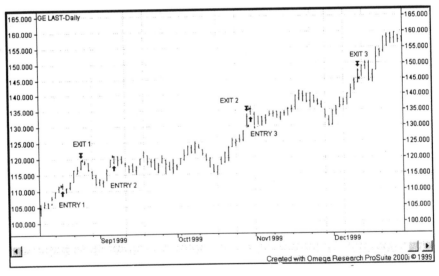

FIGURE *12-5: A TREND-FOLLOWING EXAMPLE*

TradeStation Strategy Performance Report - GAP-2H GE-Daily
(8/5/99-1/1/00)

Performance Summary: All Trades

Total Net Profit	$26.44	Open position P/L	$0.00
Gross Profit	$26.44	Gross Loss	$0.00
Total # of trades	3	Percent profitable	100.00%
Number winning trades	3	Number losing trades	0
Largest winning trade	$9.50	Largest losing trade	$0.00
Average winning trade	$8.81	Average losing trade	$0.00
Ratio avg win/avg loss	100.00	Avg trade (win & loss)	8.81
Max consec. Winners	3	Max consec. losers	0
Avg # bars in winners	23	Avg # bars in losers	0
Max intraday drawdown		($7.31)	
Profit Factor	100.00	Max # contracts held	1

FIGURE 12-6: BACK-TESTING RESULTS FOR THE TREND FOLLOWING EXAMPLE

PATTERN GROUPS AND SUB-GROUPS

Trading system models build by grouping a large number of price patterns, called PCM here, exhibit some very interesting properties. Each individual pattern or a group of patterns can be thought of as a sub-trading system model. There is virtually an infinite number of ways that this grouping can take place, depending on selected common characteristics of the patterns involved. Then different sub-groups can be grouped further to form new groups, and so on. The possibilities are endless, indeed.

The practical ramifications from this property of price patterns are many and allow increased flexibility of managing trading risk and position size. As an example, one possible grouping may be based on the bar sequence length of the patterns involved as follows:

Group 1: Based on bar sequence length.

Sub-group 1: Patterns with bar sequence length of   3
Sub-group 2:   ===   4
Sub-group 3:   ===   5
Sub-group 4:   ===   6

The above may be called a Bar Sequence Grouping, (BSG). Another possible grouping is by profit target and stop-loss magnitude:

Group 2: Based on profit target and stop-loss.

Sub-group 5: Patterns with profit target less or equal to 4%
Sub-group 6: Patterns with profit target greater than 4%
Sub-group 7: Patterns with stop-loss less or equal 4%
Sub-group 8: Patterns with stop-loss greater to 4%

The above may be called a Profit and Loss Grouping (PLG). Typically, groups are not mutually exclusive; *i.e.* members of one group can be also members of another.

Grouping and sub-grouping allow for increased flexibility in pattern trading. However, correct application of this type of systems requires careful back testing and analysis in order to determine the risk/reward parameters. Proper use of sub-groups can result in increased profitability at reduced risk. I will omit a more rigorous discussion on this subject, at this point, as it is slated to be the subject of a future publication.

CHAPTER THIRTEEN

MONEY MANAGEMENT

Money Management is a very important subject that cannot be omitted from any discussion on trading. Many traders focus exclusively on the development of a trading system model and often overlook even the basic application of money management that deals with the determination of the amount of capital required to trade a system properly. The result is often an inadequately funded system that may result in trading losses, regardless of its tested profitability.

Moreover, many traders and trading system developers attempt to devise complicated procedures for varying trading risk depending on parameters such as the system equity growth or drawdown. The objective is to maximize net profit and/or minimize losses. One important parameter that is often overlooked in such attempts is that the trading system equity growth, for instance, is not an independent variable but a complex function of the trading system output itself. By "feeding back" this complex function into the system trading logic, a completely new and very different system is created that needs to be analyzed and tested from start. A certain fallacy that may be present here is that a trading system that is back-tested profitable will certainly remain as such even after those ad-hoc changes are made, or even show increased profitability. The real problem appears, however, in the case that the trading system model actual performance deviates for the back-tested one. The resulting losses in that case may amount to multiples of the original system, the one without the "feed-back." Therefore, any attempts to vary risk should be made only after a careful consideration of the parameters involved in the trading system model.

From a money management viewpoint, trading is the act of managing risk. The objective of every trader must be to get the maximum possible profit while assuming the lowest possible risk. In general, two different types of trading systems may be defined:

Constant Risk Trading Systems, (CRTS), are those that assume the same level of risk every time that a new position is established. This is the most common way that short-term and day trading systems are used in practice. The risk, as a percentage of the initial trading capital, may be determined as the ratio of the dollar stop-loss assigned per trade divided by the initial trading capital. For instance, if the dollar stop-loss is $2,000 and the initial trading capital $100,000, then the risk is 0.02, or 2% of the initial trading capital. One useful conclusion from this simple calculation is the fact that it would take 50 consecutive losing trades, at $2,000 lost per-trade, to completely wipe out the initial trading capital, not including commissions paid. Experienced traders often recommend that the risk per trade not to exceed a very small percentage of the initial trading capital, in the order of 1% to 3%. However, most traders, especially the novice ones, totally ignore this recommendation and trade without knowing the level of risk taken. The result is well known and need not be re-mentioned here...

Variable Risk Trading Systems, (VRTS), use various methods to vary the risk assumed per position when deemed appropriate. This is practically accomplished by varying the number of shares bought or sold for a given initial trading capital or by adjusting the profit target and stop-loss levels, or both, according to some pre-determined procedure. Estimation of the risk-reward parameters of such trading systems is not a simple task. Proper application of VRTS methods requires their correct modeling and back-testing as an integral part of the trading system model in use. An example of that is the use of successive, coincident and clustered trading signals discussed in chapter twelve. Those can be used, as previously mentioned, to vary the number of shares traded and/or to move the profit target and stop-loss to new price levels.

DETERMINATION OF INITIAL TRADING CAPITAL

Underestimation of the initial capital required to trade a mechanical system may result in premature termination of trading due to mounting losses. This happens when the trading capital at hand is inadequate to cover the actual drawdown of a trading system. Since the drawdown can never be known in advance, but only its expected value obtained through back-testing, it is recommended to select a constant risk level and calculate the required initial trading capital requirement per contract according to the formula:

$$M = \frac{S}{R} \qquad\qquad (1)$$

Where:

M: the initial trading capital requirement, in $.

R: the risk level per trade, in decimal ranging from 0 to 1.0.

S: the stop-loss per trade, in $.

If, for instance, a risk level of 0.02, or 2% is desired, and a stop-loss of $5,000 per trade, the initial trading capital requirement is $250,000. If the trader decides to risk the same amount of $5,000 per trade but has only $50,000 in the trading account then, the effective risk is 10%, as it can be calculated from equation (1) above. In this case, it will take only 10 consecutive losing trades to completely wipe out the trading account, as opposed to 50 losing trades that were required before.

Equation (1) applies to trading systems where the stop-loss per trade is defined in advance and remains constant. This is the typical case in short-term and day trading system application. The shortcoming of this method is that a losing trade does not always generate a dollar loss equal to the stop-loss, a fact well known to all traders. Adverse market conditions can result in higher losses due to "fast" market conditions, illiquid markets or gap openings. Nevertheless, in the case of short-term trading systems models that generate a sufficiently high number of trading signals, the longer term variations in equity from these adverse market conditions tend to be counter balanced by favorable conditions that generate higher profits than the selected profit target.

RISK (%)	STOP-LOSS ($)	INITIAL TRADING CAPITAL ($)
	1,000	100,000
1	2,000	200,000
	5,000	500,000
	1,000	50,000
2	2,000	100,000
	5,000	250,000
4	1,000	25,000
	2,000	50,000
	5,000	125,000

TABLE 13-1: INITIAL TRADING CAPITAL REQUIREMENTS

Table 13-1 shows some examples of the initial trading capital requirement, for various levels of the stop-loss and risk levels in the case of constant risk trading systems.

The next step is to determine how much of the trading capital must be allocated in each new trade. For this purpose, the dollar stop-loss per trade, S in equation 1, can further be expressed as:

$$S = Ts \times m \qquad\qquad (2)$$

Where:

Ts: is the percent stop-loss

m: is the portion of the initial trading capital used in opening a new position.

Combining equation 1 and 2, yields:

$$M = \frac{Ts \times m}{R} \qquad\qquad (3)$$

Solving equation 3 for m yields:

$$m = M \times \frac{R}{Ts} \qquad\qquad (4)$$

or

$$\frac{m}{M} = \frac{R}{Ts} \qquad\qquad (5)$$

Equation 4 gives the portion of the initial trading capital M, denoted as m, that must be allocated when taking a new position with a percent stop-loss Ts, in order to maintain a constant risk level R. Furthermore, form equation 5, the following may be noticed:

a). The full initial trading capital may be invested in a new trade only when the risk equals to the stop-loss.

b). As the stop-loss increases, the amount that can be allocated is reduced to the appropriate fraction of the initial trading capital.

c). Full allocation depends only on the ratio of risk to stop-loss and not on the corresponding actual magnitudes.

The excess capital generated, E, may be defined as follows:

$$E = M - m \qquad\qquad (6)$$

and equals the difference between the initial trading capital and that portion of it used per trade.

Combining equations 4 and 6 above, yields:

$$E = M - M \times \frac{R}{Ts} \quad \text{or} \quad E = M \times \left[1 - \frac{R}{Ts}\right] \qquad (7)$$

Equation 7 gives the excess capital available as a function of the initial trading capital M, the risk R and the percent stop-loss, Ts. It may be seen that E becomes zero when the ratio of risk to stop-loss is unity and approaches the value of the initial trading capital as the ratio approaches zero. This can also be seen from figure 13-1, a graph of the excess capital E as a function of the ratio of risk to stop-loss.

The practical use of equation 7 is of significant importance to the application of short-term and day trading systems for trading stocks. It shows that any attempt to minimize the risk assumed per trade should be followed by a proportional reduction in the value of the percent stop-loss, in order to utilize fully the initial trading capital available. This may be kind of obvious. What may not be obvious, and it is noticed by equation 7, is that excess capital is created when the stop-loss is increased in proportion to the risk taken. Since the excess capital is not invested, the intention should be to minimize it as much as possible, while maintaining the same level of risk. However, for risk levels in the order of 1% or 2%, it may be difficult to design trading systems models that will successfully implement this low level of stop-loss. This is due to the high volatility of stock market prices. Small values of the stop-loss result in very low profitability when volatility is present. A reasonable range for the stop-loss is between 4% and 7%. As a result, the creation of excess capital is often inevitable, if one desires a low risk level. In those cases the excess capital, as a percentage of the initial trading capital, is calculated as follows:

Example 1:

R = 2% , Ts = 4%

Then form equation 7: $E = M \times \left[1 - \dfrac{2}{4}\right] = M \times 0.5$ or

E is 50% of M. This means that 50% of the initial trading capital stays aside in order to maintain a risk of 2% per trade.

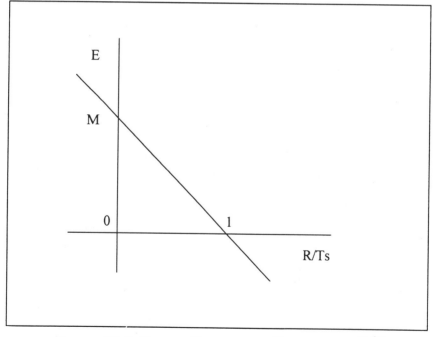

FIGURE 13-1: EXCESS CAPITAL AS A FUNCTION OF R/Ts

Example 2:

R = 3% , Ts = 5%

Then form equation 7: $E = M \times \left[1 - \dfrac{3}{5}\right] = M \times 0.4$ or

E is 40% of M. This means that only 60% of the initial trading capital stays is used in order to maintain the risk of 2% per trade.

As a final note, equation 7 indicates that the stop-loss Ts can never get smaller than the risk, R. If this happens, the excess capital E is negative, *i.e.* the trading account is under-funded for the required risk. That would happen, for instance if the risk were 4% and the stop-loss 2%. In this example, the allocated capital required is double the initial trading capital. Therefore, if only half of the required capital is used, the effective risk is reduced to a level equal to that of the stop-loss. In other words, the maximum risk that can be assumed equals to the stop-loss, in percentage terms. Likewise, the initial trading capital is fully utilized when the risk per trade equals the stop-loss.

THE USE OF MARGIN

In the case that a margin account is used, the trader must insure that the maximum equity drawdown will never exceed the cash portion of the initial trading capital. Let:

M = the initial trading capital, in $.

D_R = maximum expected drawdown, in $.

f = a safety factor multiplier.

g = the margin level in percentage.

Then:

$$\text{Cash account portion} = g \times M$$

The following is required:

$$g \times M > f \times D_R \quad \text{or}$$

$$M > f \times \frac{D_R}{g} \qquad (8)$$

As an example, if the maximum drawdown is $10,000 and the margin 50% then, for f set to one, the initial trading capital, as given by equation 8, must be greater than:

$$M > \frac{\$10,000}{0.5} \quad \text{or } M > \$20,000$$

The presence of the safety factor f serves the purpose of accounting for a possible future increase in the drawdown amount calculated by the back-testing of a trading system model. Experience has shown that trading systems tend to generate much higher drawdown during actual trading and a number of, at least, 2 is recommended for f.

As an example, let us consider a situation with the following parameters:

Risk:	$R =$	0.02 or 2%
Stop:	$S =$	$2,000
Drawdown:	$D_R =$	$20,000
Margin:	$g =$	50%
Factor:	$f =$	2

Then, from equation (1):

$$M = \frac{\$2,000}{0.02} = \$100,000$$

and from equation (8):

$$M > 2 \times \frac{\$20,000}{0.5} = \$80,000$$

The conclusion is that the initial trading capital requirement of $100,000 is adequate to cover a possible future doubling of the maximum drawdown, when a 50% margin is used. If the safety factor is increased to 3 then, from equation 8:

$$M > 3 \times \frac{\$20,000}{0.5} = \$120,000$$

In this case, the initial trading capital of $100,000 is not enough to cover a possible three-fold increase in the maximum drawdown and it must be increased to, at least, $120,000, meaning that at least $60,000 in cash is required to start with.

The figures derived from equation 8 are decisively influenced by the selection of the magnitude of the factor f. Increasing the value of f results in increased initial trading capital requirements and reduced returns but also reduced risk, in terms of equity maximum drawdown and volatility. Decreasing the value of f results in reduced initial trading capital requirements and increased returns but higher equity maximum drawdown and volatility. There is no procedure to determine f, *a priori*, because its optimum value depends on the actual future trading system drawdown that is simply not known in advance. The selection must be made arbitrarily and based on experience. Numbers between 1.5 and 2.5 seem to give good results.

SECTION FOUR

PATTERN LIBRARY

Chapter Fourteen

Pattern Library Conventions

In this chapter, guidelines for using the library of stock patterns are provided. These patterns have been found using the automatic pattern search procedures (APS) described in chapter 6. Each pattern in the library is defined by the following parameters:

Pattern Type:

This is the pattern type, as defined in chapter 3. In this section only the simplest type of exact patterns is included for simplicity reasons.

Entry Signal Type:

There are two choices, long or short. The pattern must be used for taking a position in the direction specified.

Order Entry Point:

That can be either the close of the day that the pattern formation is completed or the open of the next day.

171

APPLICABLE STOCKS:

This is a list of stocks that the pattern applies to and for which the back-testing results are also shown. Although the pattern may be applicable to trading other stocks, not listed in the library, correct application must be preceded by careful analysis and back-testing.

PROFIT TARGET:

Next to each stock the appropriate profit target is listed in percentage terms. This profit target refers to the entry price and must be used in conjunction with the specific pattern. Changing the profit target requires re-testing the pattern's historical performance to determine how the profitability is affected.

PROTECTIVE STOP:

Next to each stock the appropriate stop-loss is also listed in percentage terms. This stop-loss refers to the entry price and must be used in conjunction with the specific pattern. Changing the stop-loss requires re-testing the pattern's historical performance to determine how the profitability is affected.

BAR SEQUENCE LENGTH:

This is the pattern length in bars.

BAR SEQUENCE:

The bar sequence of each pattern is given in order to specify which parameters are included from each bar that forms it.

GRAPHICAL REPRESENTATION:

Each pattern graphical representation is also given. The notation used is demonstrated below with an example.

Figure 14-1 shows an example of a pattern formed by 4 chart bars. Every bar is labeled, above its high, starting from 0 for the most recent, which is also the bar that the pattern formation is completed.

For each bar, j, the following notation is used:

H[j] = High of the j bar
L[j] = Low of the j bar
C[j] = Close of the j bar
O[j] = Open of the j bar,   j = 0,1,2,3

The arrows placed on each bar denote the quantities that appear in the bar sequence. Then, according to the graphic example on figure 14-1, the following quantities must be included:

Bar 0: C[0]
    1: H[1], L[1], O[1], C[1]
    2: H[2], L[2]
    3: H[3], C[3]

The bar sequence of the pattern can include only the quantities labeled by the arrows. The remaining quantities are not used and, therefore, their corresponding actual position in the pattern formation can be anywhere and does not play any role in the pattern trading rules.

The bar sequence for the example in figure 14-1 is:

$$S = \{(C_0), (H_1, L_1, O_1, C_1), (H_2, L_2), (H_3, C_3)\}$$

This sequence has a length of 4 bars. For the first bar, only the close is considered as a parameter, for the second the high, low, open and close, for the third the high and low and for the forth the high and close.

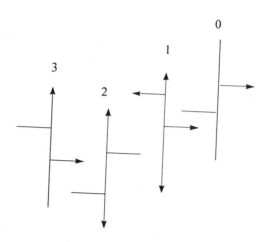

FIGURE 14-1: EXAMPLE OF PATTERN GRAPHICAL REPRESENTATION

EASYLANGUAGE CODE:

The EasyLanguage code that is required to back-test or implement for trading is shown for each pattern.

Back Testing Results:

For each stock listed for each pattern, the back-testing results are shown for a specified testing period.

Stock Universe Considered by the Pattern Library

Below is the comprehensive list of all stocks considered in the back-testing of the patterns shown in this section. It includes issues from most popular market sectors, both NYSE and NASDAQ listed.

Symbol	Description	Exchange
AAPL	Apple Computer Inc	NASDAQ
AMZN	Amazon.com Inc	NASDAQ
AXP	American Express Co	NYSE
BAC	Bank of America Corp	NYSE
C	Citigroup Inc	NYSE
CA	Computer Associates	NYSE
CAT	Caterpillar Inc	NYSE
CHV	Chevron Corp	NYSE
CMGI	CMGI Inc	NASDAQ
DD	Du Pont	NYSE
DIS	Disney	NYSE
EBAY	eBay Inc	NASDAQ
GE	General Electric Co	NYSE
GM	General Motors Corp	NYSE
GTW	Gateway Inc	NYSE
HD	Home Depot, Inc	NYSE
HWP	Hewlett-Packard Co	NYSE
IBM	Inter. Business Machines	NYSE
INTC	Intel Corp	NASDAQ
JNJ	Johnson&Johnson	NYSE
JPM	Morgan (JP) & Co Inc	NYSE
KM	K-Mart	NYSE
KO	Coca Cola Co	NYSE
MO	Philip Morris	NYSE
MRK	Merk & Co Inc	NYSE
MSFT	Microsoft Corp	NASDAQ
ORCL	Oracle Corp	NASDAQ
PG	Proctor & Gamble Co	NYSE
S	Sears Roebuck Co	NYSE
SUNW	Sun Microsystems Inc	NASDAQ
T	AT&T Corp	NYSE
WMT	Wal-Mart Stores Inc	NYSE

CHAPTER FIFTEEN

STOCK PATTERNS
N-V Pattern

Pattern Type: Exact

Entry Signal Type: Long

Order Entry Point: Open of tomorrow

Applicable Stocks:

Symbol	Profit Target %	Stop-loss %
AXP	7	7
BAC	4	4
C	9	9
CAT	7	7
DIS	8	8
GE	7	7
GM	5	5
GTW	4	4
HD	7	7
HWP	6	6
IBM	6	6
INTC	8	8
JNJ	7	7
KO	5	5
MO	4	4
MSFT	7	7
ORCL	2	2
WMT	8	8

Bar Sequence Length: 4

Bar Sequence: $S = \{(C_0), (C_1), (C_2), (C_3)\}$

Graphical Representation:

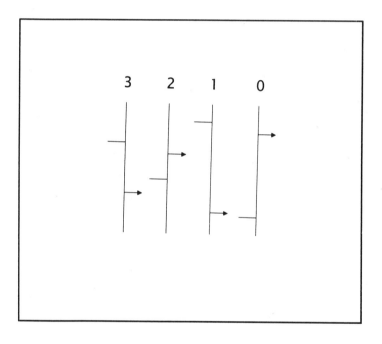

EASY LANGUAGE CODE

```
{**************************************************
Description   : N-V Pattern Entry Signal
Developed By : Michael Harris
**************************************************}


if c[0] > c[2] and c[2] > c[3] and c[3] > c[1] then
          buy  ("N-V") next bar on the open;




{**************************************************
Description   : N-V Pattern Long Exit Signal
Developed By : Michael Harris
Comments: ptarget and stopl are in percentage terms
**************************************************}

variables: profitprice(0), stopprice(0);
input: ptarget(0), stopl(0);

profitprice = entryprice*(1+ptarget/100);
stopprice = entryprice*(1-stopl/100);

if marketposition =1 then begin
        exitlong ("N-V Exit") at profitprice limit;
        exitlong ("N-V Stop") at stopprice stop;
end;
```

TradeStation Strategy Performance Report - N-V AXP-Daily
(1/2/90-1/31/00)

Performance Summary: All Trades

Total Net Profit $763.38		Open position P/L	$0.00
Gross Profit $1,684.43		Gross Loss	($921.04)
Total # of trades 36		Percent profitable	63.89%
Number winning trades 23		Number losing trades	13
Largest winning trade	$88.30	Largest losing trade	($77.60)
Average winning trade	$73.24	Average losing trade	($70.85)
Ratio avg win/avg loss	1.03	Avg trade (win & loss)	$21.21
Max consec. Winners	6	Max consec. losers	2
Avg # bars in winners	20	Avg # bars in losers	16
Max intraday drawdown		($207.94)	
Profit Factor	1.83	Max # contracts held	59

TradeStation Strategy Performance Report - N-V BAC-Daily
(1/3/90-2/1/00)

Performance Summary: All Trades

Total Net Profit $253.64		Open position P/L	$0.00
Gross Profit $626.46		Gross Loss	($372.82)
Total # of trades 24		Percent profitable	62.50%
Number winning trades 15		Number losing trades	9
Largest winning trade	$48.00	Largest losing trade	($45.60)
Average winning trade	$41.76	Average losing trade	($41.42)
Ratio avg win/avg loss	1.01	Avg trade (win & loss)	$10.57
Max consec. Winners	5	Max consec. losers	2
Avg # bars in winners	5	Avg # bars in losers	11
Max intraday drawdown		($98.73)	
Profit Factor	1.68	Max # contracts held	81

TradeStation Strategy Performance Report - N-V C-Daily
(1/3/94-1/31/00)

Performance Summary: All Trades

Total Net Profit	$476.30	Open position P/L	$0.00
Gross Profit	$930.68	Gross Loss	($454.37)
Total # of trades	15	Percent profitable	66.67%
Number winning trades	$10	Number losing trades	5
Largest winning trade	$106.99	Largest losing trade	($93.75)
Average winning trade	$93.07	Average losing trade	($90.87)
Ratio avg win/avg loss	1.02	Avg trade (win & loss)	$31.75
Max consec. Winners	6	Max consec. losers	2
Avg # bars in winners	20	Avg # bars in losers	27
Max intraday drawdown		($248.38)	
Profit Factor	2.05	Max # contracts held	127

TradeStation Strategy Performance Report - N-V CAT-Daily
(1/2/90-1/31/00)

Performance Summary: All Trades

Total Net Profit	$579.84	Open position P/L	$0.00
Gross Profit	$1,363.33	Gross Loss	($783.49)
Total # of trades	29	Percent profitable	65.52%
Number winning trades	19	Number losing trades	10
Largest winning trade	$79.38	Largest losing trade	($131.28)
Average winning trade	$71.75	Average losing trade	($78.35)
Ratio avg win/avg loss	.92	Avg trade (win & loss)	$19.99
Max consec. Winners	5	Max consec. losers	3
Avg # bars in winners	21	Avg # bars in losers	11
Max intraday drawdown		($224.07)	
Profit Factor	1.74	Max # contracts held	97

TradeStation Strategy Performance Report - N-V DIS-Daily
(1/2/90-1/31/00)

Performance Summary: All Trades

Total Net Profit	$748.99	Open position P/L	$0.00
Gross Profit	$1,496.36	Gross Loss	($747.37)
Total # of trades	27	Percent profitable	66.67%
Number winning trades	18	Number losing trades	9
Largest winning trade	$93.40	Largest losing trade	($89.78)
Average winning trade	$83.13	Average losing trade	($83.04)
Ratio avg win/avg loss	1.00	Avg trade (win & loss)	$27.74
Max consec. Winners	6	Max consec. losers	3
Avg # bars in winners	25	Avg # bars in losers	34
Max intraday drawdown		($366.29)	
Profit Factor	2.00	Max # contracts held	133

TradeStation Strategy Performance Report - N-V GE-Daily
(1/2/90-1/31/00)

Performance Summary: All Trades

Total Net Profit	$628.03	Open position P/L	$0.00
Gross Profit	$1,188.80	Gross Loss	($560.77)
Total # of trades	25	Percent profitable	68.00%
Number winning trades	17	Number losing trades	8
Largest winning trade	$74.78	Largest losing trade	($76.14)
Average winning trade	$69.93	Average losing trade	($70.10)
Ratio avg win/avg loss	1.00	Avg trade (win & loss)	$25.12
Max consec. Winners	5	Max consec. losers	2
Avg # bars in winners	37	Avg # bars in losers	25
Max intraday drawdown		($148.33)	
Profit Factor	2.12	Max # contracts held	57

TradeStation Strategy Performance Report - N-V GM-Daily
(1/2/90-1/31/00)

Performance Summary: All Trades

Total Net Profit	$377.27	Open position P/L	$0.00
Gross Profit	$987.07	Gross Loss	($609.80)
Total # of trades	32	Percent profitable	62.50%
Number winning trades	20	Number losing trades	12
Largest winning trade	$69.41	Largest losing trade	($55.70)
Average winning trade	$49.35	Average losing trade	($50.82)
Ratio avg win/avg loss	.97	Avg trade (win & loss)	$11.79
Max consec. Winners	5	Max consec. losers	3
Avg # bars in winners	7	Avg # bars in losers	14
Max intraday drawdown		($197.16)	
Profit Factor	1.62	Max # contracts held	37

TradeStation Strategy Performance Report -N-V GTW-Daily
(12/8/93-1/31/00)

Performance Summary: All Trades

Total Net Profit	$455.40	Open position P/L	$0.00
Gross Profit	$675.53	Gross Loss	($220.13)
Total # of trades	17	Percent profitable	70.59%
Number winning trades	12	Number losing trades	5
Largest winning trade	$95.98	Largest losing trade	($46.88)
Average winning trade	$56.29	Average losing trade	($44.03)
Ratio avg win/avg loss	1.28	Avg trade (win & loss)	$23.95
Max consec. Winners	7	Max consec. losers	2
Avg # bars in winners	2	Avg # bars in losers	3
Max intraday drawdown		($135.12)	
Profit Factor	3.07	Max # contracts held	190

TradeStation Strategy Performance Report -N-V HD-Daily (1/2/90-1/31/00)

Performance Summary: All Trades

Total Net Profit	$693.06	Open position P/L	$0.00
Gross Profit	$1393.11	Gross Loss	($700.05)
Total # of trades	27	Percent profitable	66.67%
Number winning trades	18	Number losing trades	9
Largest winning trade	$100.38	Largest losing trade	($100.51)
Average winning trade	$77.39	Average losing trade	($77.78)
Ratio avg win/avg loss	1.00	Avg trade (win & loss)	$25.67
Max consec. Winners	7	Max consec. losers	2
Avg # bars in winners	14	Avg # bars in losers	16
Max intraday drawdown		($206.49)	
Profit Factor	1.99	Max # contracts held	377

TradeStation Strategy Performance Report -N-V HWP-Daily (1/2/90-1/31/00)

Performance Summary: All Trades

Total Net Profit	$862.13	Open position P/L	$0.00
Gross Profit	$1,560.29	Gross Loss	($698.16)
Total # of trades	36	Percent profitable	69.44%
Number winning trades	25	Number losing trades	11
Largest winning trade	$90.89	Largest losing trade	($81.14)
Average winning trade	$62.41	Average losing trade	($63.47)
Ratio avg win/avg loss	.98	Avg trade (win & loss)	$23.95
Max consec. Winners	5	Max consec. losers	3
Avg # bars in winners	10	Avg # bars in losers	8
Max intraday drawdown		($241.15)	
Profit Factor	2.23	Max # contracts held	90

TradeStation Strategy Performance Report - N-V IBM-Daily
(1/2/90-1/31/00)

Performance Summary: All Trades

Total Net Profit	$680.90	Open position P/L	$0.00
Gross Profit	$1,267.98	Gross Loss	($587.07)
Total # of trades	29	Percent profitable	68.97%
Number winning trades	20	Number losing trades	9
Largest winning trade	$77.00	Largest losing trade	($93.75)
Average winning trade	$63.40	Average losing trade	($65.23)
Ratio avg win/avg loss	.97	Avg trade (win & loss)	$23.48
Max consec. Winners	12	Max consec. losers	2
Avg # bars in winners	12	Avg # bars in losers	10
Max intraday drawdown		($176.96)	
Profit Factor	2.16	Max # contracts held	72

TradeStation Strategy Performance Report - N-V INTC-Daily
(1/2/90-1/31/00)

Performance Summary: All Trades

Total Net Profit	$1,232.07	Open position P/L	$0.00
Gross Profit	$1,977.93	Gross Loss	($745.85)
Total # of trades	32	Percent profitable	71.88%
Number winning trades	23	Number losing trades	9
Largest winning trade	$108.45	Largest losing trade	($95.12)
Average winning trade	$86.00	Average losing trade	($82.87)
Ratio avg win/avg loss	1.04	Avg trade (win & loss)	$38.50
Max consec. Winners	8	Max consec. losers	3
Avg # bars in winners	13	Avg # bars in losers	10
Max intraday drawdown		($272.58)	
Profit Factor	2.65	Max # contracts held	422

TradeStation Strategy Performance Report - N-V JNJ-Daily (1/2/90-1/31/00)

Performance Summary: All Trades

Total Net Profit	$659.47	Open position P/L	$0.00
Gross Profit	$1,438.90	Gross Loss	($779.43)
Total # of trades	31	Percent profitable	64.52%
Number winning trades	20	Number losing trades	11
Largest winning trade	$83.97	Largest losing trade	($77.18)
Average winning trade	$71.94	Average losing trade	($70.86)
Ratio avg win/avg loss	1.02	Avg trade (win & loss)	$21.27
Max consec. Winners	6	Max consec. losers	3
Avg # bars in winners	26	Avg # bars in losers	14
Max intraday drawdown		($269.23)	
Profit Factor	1.85	Max # contracts held	68

TradeStation Strategy Performance Report - N-V KO-Daily (1/2/90-1/31/00)

Performance Summary: All Trades

Total Net Profit	$628.47	Open position P/L	$0.00
Gross Profit	$1,052.48	Gross Loss	($424.01)
Total # of trades	28	Percent profitable	71.43%
Number winning trades	20	Number losing trades	8
Largest winning trade	$62.70	Largest losing trade	($69.30)
Average winning trade	$52.62	Average losing trade	($53.00)
Ratio avg win/avg loss	.99	Avg trade (win & loss)	$22.45
Max consec. Winners	8	Max consec. losers	2
Avg # bars in winners	18	Avg # bars in losers	19
Max intraday drawdown		($98.13)	
Profit Factor	2.48	Max # contracts held	110

TradeStation Strategy Performance Report - N-V MO-Daily (1/2/90-1/31/00)

Performance Summary: All Trades

Total Net Profit	$458.75	Open position P/L	$0.00
Gross Profit	$943.94	Gross Loss	($485.19)
Total # of trades	31	Percent profitable	67.74%
Number winning trades	21	Number losing trades	10
Largest winning trade	$94.08	Largest losing trade	($69.20)
Average winning trade	$44.95	Average losing trade	($48.52)
Ratio avg win/avg loss	.93	Avg trade (win & loss)	$14.80
Max consec. Winners	6	Max consec. losers	3
Avg # bars in winners	8	Avg # bars in losers	4
Max intraday drawdown		($202.94)	
Profit Factor	1.95	Max # contracts held	71

TradeStation Strategy Performance Report - N-V MSFT-Daily (1/2/90-1/31/00)

Performance Summary: All Trades

Total Net Profit	$906.83	Open position P/L	$0.00
Gross Profit	$1,609.57	Gross Loss	($702.74)
Total # of trades	30	Percent profitable	70.00%
Number winning trades	21	Number losing trades	9
Largest winning trade	$106.18	Largest losing trade	($105.40)
Average winning trade	$76.65	Average losing trade	($78.08)
Ratio avg win/avg loss	.98	Avg trade (win & loss)	$30.23
Max consec. Winners	11	Max consec. losers	2
Avg # bars in winners	9	Avg # bars in losers	18
Max intraday drawdown		($216.04)	
Profit Factor	2.29	Max # contracts held	553

TradeStation Strategy Performance Report - N-V ORCL-Daily
(1/2/90-1/31/00)

Performance Summary: All Trades

Total Net Profit	$836.53	Open position P/L	$0.00
Gross Profit	$1,610.13	Gross Loss	($773.60)
Total # of trades	43	Percent profitable	62.79%
Number winning trades	27	Number losing trades	16
Largest winning trade	$229.04	Largest losing trade	($128.87)
Average winning trade	$59.63	Average losing trade	($48.35)
Ratio avg win/avg loss	1.23	Avg trade (win & loss)	$19.45
Max consec. Winners	5	Max consec. losers	2
Avg # bars in winners	4	Avg # bars in losers	4
Max intraday drawdown		($267.08)	
Profit Factor	2.08	Max # contracts held	2,688

TradeStation Strategy Performance Report - N-V WMT-Daily
(1/2/90-1/31/00)

Performance Summary: All Trades

Total Net Profit	$768.41	Open position P/L	$0.00
Gross Profit	$1,433.48	Gross Loss	($665.07)
Total # of trades	25	Percent profitable	68.00%
Number winning trades	17	Number losing trades	8
Largest winning trade	$92.03	Largest losing trade	($86.72)
Average winning trade	$84.32	Average losing trade	($83.13)
Ratio avg win/avg loss	1.01	Avg trade (win & loss)	$30.74
Max consec. Winners	7	Max consec. losers	3
Avg # bars in winners	21	Avg # bars in losers	21
Max intraday drawdown		($356.59)	
Profit Factor	2.16	Max # contracts held	187

Gamma Pattern

Pattern Type: Exact

Entry Signal Type: Long

Order Entry Point: Open of tomorrow

Applicable Stocks:

Symbol	Profit Target %	Stop-loss %
C	6	6
CA	4	4
CAT	9	9
GE	8	8
GTW	9	9
HD	7	7
INTC	6	6
JNJ	7	7
JPM	5	5
KO	5	5
MCD	7	7
MRK	7	7
MSFT	4	4
PG	5	5
T	T	7
WMT	7	7

Bar Sequence Length: 4

Bar Sequence: $S = \{(C_0), (C_1), (C_2), (C_3)\}$

Graphical Representation:

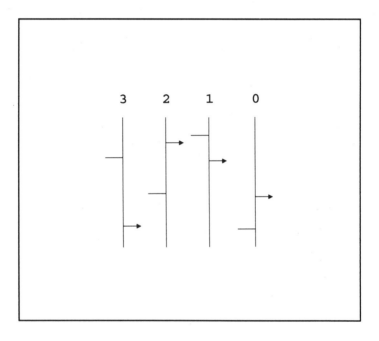

Easy Language Code

```
{**************************************************
Description   : Gamma Pattern Entry Signal
Developed By : Michael Harris
**************************************************}


if c[2] > c[1] and c[1] > c[0] and c[0] > c[3] then
            buy  ("Gamma") next bar on the open;


{**************************************************
Description   : Gamma Pattern Long Exit Signal
Developed By : Michael Harris
Comments: ptarget and stopl are in percentage terms
**************************************************}

variables: profitprice(0), stopprice(0);
input: ptarget(0), stopl(0);

profitprice = entryprice*(1+ptarget/100);
stopprice = entryprice*(1-stopl/100);

if marketposition =1 then begin
        exitlong ("Gamma Exit") at profitprice limit;
        exitlong ("Gamma Stop") at stopprice stop;
end;
```

TradeStation Strategy Performance Report - Gamma C-Daily (1/3/94-1/31/00)

Performance Summary: All Trades

Total Net Profit	$681.79	Open position P/L	$0.00
Gross Profit	$1,578.28	Gross Loss	($896.49)
Total # of trades	38	Percent profitable	63.16%
Number winning trades	24	Number losing trades	14
Largest winning trade	$86.85	Largest losing trade	($87.12)
Average winning trade	$65.76	Average losing trade	($64.03)
Ratio avg win/avg loss	1.03	Avg trade (win & loss)	$17.94
Max consec. Winners	7	Max consec. losers	2
Avg # bars in winners	10	Avg # bars in losers	7
Max intraday drawdown		($226.71)	
Profit Factor	1.76	Max # contracts held	138

TradeStation Strategy Performance Report - Gamma CA-Daily (1/3/90-2/1/00)

Performance Summary: All Trades

Total Net Profit	$1,203.07	Open position P/L	$0.00
Gross Profit	$2,370.63	Gross Loss	($1,167.56)
Total # of trades	67	Percent profitable	68.66%
Number winning trades	46	Number losing trades	21
Largest winning trade	$112.38	Largest losing trade	($122.66)
Average winning trade	$51.54	Average losing trade	($55.60)
Ratio avg win/avg loss	.93	Avg trade (win & loss)	$17.96
Max consec. Winners	10	Max consec. losers	3
Avg # bars in winners	4	Avg # bars in losers	3
Max intraday drawdown		($232.83)	
Profit Factor	2.03	Max # contracts held	513

TradeStation Strategy Performance Report - Gamma CAT-Daily (1/2/90-1/31/00)

Performance Summary: All Trades

Total Net Profit	$1,241.49	Open position P/L	$0.00
Gross Profit	$2,569.11	Gross Loss	($1,327.62)
Total # of trades	42	Percent profitable	66.67%
Number winning trades	28	Number losing trades	14
Largest winning trade	$101.88	Largest losing trade	($127.38)
Average winning trade	$91.75	Average losing trade	($94.83)
Ratio avg win/avg loss	.97	Avg trade (win & loss)	$29.56
Max consec. Winners	11	Max consec. losers	3
Avg # bars in winners	32	Avg # bars in losers	23
Max intraday drawdown		($391.54)	
Profit Factor	1.94	Max # contracts held	95

TradeStation Strategy Performance Report - Gamma GE-Daily (1/2/90-1/31/00)

Performance Summary: All Trades

Total Net Profit	$1,035.67	Open position P/L	$0.00
Gross Profit	$1,855.56	Gross Loss	($819.89)
Total # of trades	33	Percent profitable	69.70%
Number winning trades	23	Number losing trades	10
Largest winning trade	$87.00	Largest losing trade	($112.50)
Average winning trade	$80.68	Average losing trade	($81.99)
Ratio avg win/avg loss	.98	Avg trade (win & loss)	$31.38
Max consec. Winners	7	Max consec. losers	3
Avg # bars in winners	52	Avg # bars in losers	21
Max intraday drawdown		($237.50)	
Profit Factor	2.26	Max # contracts held	74

TradeStation Strategy Performance Report - Gamma GTW-Daily (12/8/93-1/31/00)

Performance Summary: All Trades

Total Net Profit	$1,198.04	Open position P/L	$0.00
Gross Profit	$2,499.59	Gross Loss	($1,301.55)
Total # of trades	40	Percent profitable	65.00%
Number winning trades	26	Number losing trades	14
Largest winning trade	$140.13	Largest losing trade	($103.54)
Average winning trade	$96.14	Average losing trade	($92.97)
Ratio avg win/avg loss	1.03	Avg trade (win & loss)	$29.95
Max consec. Winners	7	Max consec. losers	4
Avg # bars in winners	6	Avg # bars in losers	5
Max intraday drawdown		($489.85)	
Profit Factor	1.92	Max # contracts held	293

TradeStation Strategy Performance Report - Gamma HD-Daily (1/2/90-1/31/00)

Performance Summary: All Trades

Total Net Profit	$1,603.62	Open position P/L	$0.00
Gross Profit	$2,568.40	Gross Loss	($964.78)
Total # of trades	46	Percent profitable	71.74%
Number winning trades	33	Number losing trades	13
Largest winning trade	$113.03	Largest losing trade	($82.75)
Average winning trade	$77.83	Average losing trade	($74.21)
Ratio avg win/avg loss	1.05	Avg trade (win & loss)	$34.86
Max consec. Winners	8	Max consec. losers	3
Avg # bars in winners	16	Avg # bars in losers	14
Max intraday drawdown		($315.37)	
Profit Factor	2.66	Max # contracts held	445

TradeStation Strategy Performance Report - Gamma INTC-Daily (1/2/90-1/31/00)

Performance Summary: All Trades

Total Net Profit	$1,311.05	Open position P/L	$0.00
Gross Profit	$2,616.45	Gross Loss	($1,305.40)
Total # of trades	59	Percent profitable	67.80%
Number winning trades	40	Number losing trades	19
Largest winning trade	$84.07	Largest losing trade	($101.72)
Average winning trade	$65.41	Average losing trade	($68.71)
Ratio avg win/avg loss	.95	Avg trade (win & loss)	$22.22
Max consec. Winners	7	Max consec. losers	4
Avg # bars in winners	8	Avg # bars in losers	7
Max intraday drawdown		($347.72)	
Profit Factor	2.00	Max # contracts held	386

TradeStation Strategy Performance Report - Gamma JNJ-Daily (1/2/90-1/31/00)

Performance Summary: All Trades

Total Net Profit	$970.86	Open position P/L	$0.00
Gross Profit	$2,187.31	Gross Loss	($1,216.46)
Total # of trades	48	Percent profitable	64.58%
Number winning trades	31	Number losing trades	17
Largest winning trade	$75.00	Largest losing trade	($81.72)
Average winning trade	$70.56	Average losing trade	($71.56)
Ratio avg win/avg loss	.99	Avg trade (win & loss)	$20.23
Max consec. Winners	7	Max consec. losers	3
Avg # bars in winners	17	Avg # bars in losers	20
Max intraday drawdown		($320.78)	
Profit Factor	1.80	Max # contracts held	74

TradeStation Strategy Performance Report - Gamma JPM-Daily (1/2/90-1/31/00)

Performance Summary: All Trades

Total Net Profit	$952.18	Open position P/L	$0.00
Gross Profit	$1,540.24	Gross Loss	($588.07)
Total # of trades	43	Percent profitable	72.09%
Number winning trades	31	Number losing trades	12
Largest winning trade	$56.88	Largest losing trade	($52.50)
Average winning trade	$49.69	Average losing trade	($49.01)
Ratio avg win/avg loss	1.01	Avg trade (win & loss)	$22.14
Max consec. Winners	9	Max consec. losers	3
Avg # bars in winners	12	Avg # bars in losers	11
Max intraday drawdown		($151.38)	
Profit Factor	2.62	Max # contracts held	28

TradeStation Strategy Performance Report - Gamma KO-Daily (1/2/90-1/31/00)

Performance Summary: All Trades

Total Net Profit	$831.80	Open position P/L	$0.00
Gross Profit	$1,711.86	Gross Loss	($880.06)
Total # of trades	50	Percent profitable	66.00%
Number winning trades	33	Number losing trades	17
Largest winning trade	$67.49	Largest losing trade	($59.50)
Average winning trade	$51.87	Average losing trade	($51.77)
Ratio avg win/avg loss	1.00	Avg trade (win & loss)	$16.64
Max consec. Winners	11	Max consec. losers	2
Avg # bars in winners	18	Avg # bars in losers	12
Max intraday drawdown		($137.38)	
Profit Factor	1.95	Max # contracts held	115

TradeStation Strategy Performance Report - Gamma MCD-Daily (1/2/90-1/31/00)

Performance Summary: All Trades

Total Net Profit	$1,168.52	Open position P/L	$0.00
Gross Profit	$1,957.04	Gross Loss	($788.51)
Total # of trades	37	Percent profitable	70.27%
Number winning trades	26	Number losing trades	11
Largest winning trade	$116.25	Largest losing trade	($77.88)
Average winning trade	$75.27	Average losing trade	($71.68)
Ratio avg win/avg loss	1.05	Avg trade (win & loss)	$31.58
Max consec. Winners	9	Max consec. losers	3
Avg # bars in winners	24	Avg # bars in losers	17
Max intraday drawdown		($223.46)	
Profit Factor	2.48	Max # contracts held	155

TradeStation Strategy Performance Report - Gamma MRK-Daily (1/2/90-1/31/00)

Performance Summary: All Trades

Total Net Profit	$976.53	Open position P/L	$0.00
Gross Profit	$2,015.75	Gross Loss	($1,039.22)
Total # of trades	43	Percent profitable	65.12%
Number winning trades	28	Number losing trades	15
Largest winning trade	$78.51	Largest losing trade	($72.47)
Average winning trade	$71.99	Average losing trade	($69.28)
Ratio avg win/avg loss	1.04	Avg trade (win & loss)	$22.71
Max consec. Winners	7	Max consec. losers	3
Avg # bars in winners	28	Avg # bars in losers	13
Max intraday drawdown		($363.29)	
Profit Factor	1.94	Max # contracts held	76

TradeStation Strategy Performance Report - Gamma MSFT-Daily (1/2/90-1/31/00)

Performance Summary: All Trades

Total Net Profit	$1,209.45	Open position P/L	$0.00
Gross Profit	$2,409.59	Gross Loss	($1,200.14)
Total # of trades	73	Percent profitable	65.75%
Number winning trades	48	Number losing trades	25
Largest winning trade	$132.11	Largest losing trade	($72.77)
Average winning trade	$50.20	Average losing trade	($48.01)
Ratio avg win/avg loss	1.05	Avg trade (win & loss)	$16.57
Max consec. Winners	12	Max consec. losers	5
Avg # bars in winners	5	Avg # bars in losers	4
Max intraday drawdown		($378.80)	
Profit Factor	2.01	Max # contracts held	791

TradeStation Strategy Performance Report - Gamma PG-Daily (1/2/90-1/31/00)

Performance Summary: All Trades

Total Net Profit	$1,304.05	Open position P/L	$0.00
Gross Profit	$1,958.08	Gross Loss	($654.02)
Total # of trades	52	Percent profitable	75.00%
Number winning trades	39	Number losing trades	13
Largest winning trade	$55.40	Largest losing trade	($55.13)
Average winning trade	$50.21	Average losing trade	($50.31)
Ratio avg win/avg loss	1.00	Avg trade (win & loss)	$25.08
Max consec. Winners	14	Max consec. losers	3
Avg # bars in winners	13	Avg # bars in losers	14
Max intraday drawdown		($209.22)	
Profit Factor	2.99	Max # contracts held	62

TradeStation Strategy Performance Report - Gamma T-Daily
(1/2/90-1/31/00)

Performance Summary: All Trades

Total Net Profit	$900.17	Open position P/L	$0.00
Gross Profit	$1,658.44	Gross Loss	($758.27)
Total # of trades	33	Percent profitable	69.70%
Number winning trades	23	Number losing trades	10
Largest winning trade	$85.25	Largest losing trade	($120.91)
Average winning trade	$72.11	Average losing trade	($75.83)
Ratio avg win/avg loss	.95	Avg trade (win & loss)	$27.28
Max consec. Winners	11	Max consec. losers	3
Avg # bars in winners	25	Avg # bars in losers	25
Max intraday drawdown		($261.88)	
Profit Factor	2.19	Max # contracts held	66

TradeStation Strategy Performance Report - Gamma WMT-
Daily (1/2/90-1/31/00)

Performance Summary: All Trades

Total Net Profit	$1,400.60	Open position P/L	$0.00
Gross Profit	$2,294.41	Gross Loss	($893.82)
Total # of trades	42	Percent profitable	71.43%
Number winning trades	30	Number losing trades	12
Largest winning trade	$92.00	Largest losing trade	($92.48)
Average winning trade	$76.48	Average losing trade	($74.48)
Ratio avg win/avg loss	1.03	Avg trade (win & loss)	$33.35
Max consec. Winners	6	Max consec. losers	2
Avg # bars in winners	19	Avg # bars in losers	17
Max intraday drawdown		($237.18)	
Profit Factor	2.57	Max # contracts held	169

Lambda Pattern

Pattern Type: Exact

Entry Signal Type: Short

Order Entry Point: Open of tomorrow

Applicable Stocks:

Symbol	Profit Target %	Stop-loss %
AAPL	6	6
GTW	7	7
KM	2	2
SUNW	2	2
WMT	2	2
GM	3	3
IBM	1	1

Bar Sequence Length: 4

Bar Sequence: $S = \{(C_0), (C_1), (C_2), (C_3)\}$

Graphical Representation:

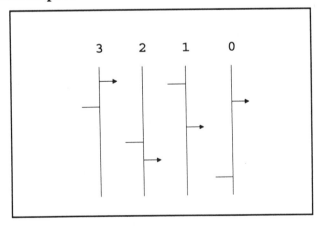

Easy Language Code

```
{**************************************************
Description : Lambda Pattern Entry Signal
Developed By : Michael Harris
**************************************************}

if c[3] > c[0] and c[0] > c[1] and c[1] > c[2] then
          Sell  ("Lambda") next bar on the open;


{**************************************************
Description   : Lambda Pattern Short Exit Signal
Developed By : Michael Harris
Comments: ptarget and stopl are in percentage terms
**************************************************}

variables: profitprice(0), stopprice(0);
input: ptarget(0), stopl(0);

profitprice = entryprice*(1-ptarget/100);
stopprice = entryprice*(1+stopl/100);

if marketposition =-1 then begin
        exitshort ("Gamma Exit")  at profitprice limit;
        exitshort ("Gamma Stop") at stopprice stop;
end;
```

TradeStation Strategy Performance Report - Lambda AAPL-
Daily (1/2/90-1/31/00)

Performance Summary: All Trades

Total Net Profit	$753.83	Open position P/L	$0.00
Gross Profit	$1,980.20	Gross Loss	($1,226.37)
Total # of trades	52	Percent profitable	61.54%
Number winning trades	32	Number losing trades	20
Largest winning trade	$89.25	Largest losing trade	($74.38)
Average winning trade	$61.88	Average losing trade	($61.32)
Ratio avg win/avg loss	1.01	Avg trade (win & loss)	$14.50
Max consec. Winners	10	Max consec. losers	3
Avg # bars in winners	6	Avg # bars in losers	6
Max intraday drawdown		($197.92)	
Profit Factor	1.61	Max # contracts held	63

TradeStation Strategy Performance Report - Lambda GM-
Daily (1/2/90-1/31/00)

Performance Summary: All Trades

Total Net Profit	$499.10	Open position P/L	$0.00
Gross Profit	$1,015.26	Gross Loss	($516.17)
Total # of trades	49	Percent profitable	67.35%
Number winning trades	33	Number losing trades	16
Largest winning trade	$36.96	Largest losing trade	($41.97)
Average winning trade	$30.77	Average losing trade	($32.26)
Ratio avg win/avg loss	.95	Avg trade (win & loss)	$10.19
Max consec. Winners	11	Max consec. losers	2
Avg # bars in winners	3	Avg # bars in losers	2
Max intraday drawdown		($131.59)	
Profit Factor	1.97	Max # contracts held	32

TradeStation Strategy Performance Report - Lambda GTW-Daily (12/8/93-1/31/00)

Performance Summary: All Trades

Total Net Profit	$847.87	Open position P/L	$0.00
Gross Profit	$1,788.47	Gross Loss	($940.60)
Total # of trades	34	Percent profitable	64.71%
Number winning trades	22	Number losing trades	12
Largest winning trade	$115.58	Largest losing trade	($101.25)
Average winning trade	$81.29	Average losing trade	($78.38)
Ratio avg win/avg loss	1.04	Avg trade (win & loss)	$24.94
Max consec. Winners	7	Max consec. losers	3
Avg # bars in winners	5	Avg # bars in losers	3
Max intraday drawdown		($329.31)	
Profit Factor	1.90	Max # contracts held	340

TradeStation Strategy Performance Report - Lambda IBM-Daily (1/2/90-1/31/00)

Performance Summary: All Trades

Total Net Profit	$332.05	Open position P/L	$0.00
Gross Profit	$637.55	Gross Loss	($305.50)
Total # of trades	56	Percent profitable	64.29%
Number winning trades	36	Number losing trades	20
Largest winning trade	$94.59	Largest losing trade	($31.86)
Average winning trade	$17.71	Average losing trade	($15.27)
Ratio avg win/avg loss	1.16	Avg trade (win & loss)	$5.93
Max consec. Winners	7	Max consec. losers	7
Avg # bars in winners	1	Avg # bars in losers	1
Max intraday drawdown		($129.85)	
Profit Factor	2.09	Max # contracts held	81

TradeStation Strategy Performance Report - Lambda KM-Daily (1/2/90-1/31/00)

Performance Summary: All Trades

Total Net Profit	$404.17	Open position P/L	$0.00
Gross Profit	$668.06	Gross Loss	($263.90)
Total # of trades	31	Percent profitable	74.19%
Number winning trades	23	Number losing trades	8
Largest winning trade	$64.50	Largest losing trade	($58.40)
Average winning trade	$29.05	Average losing trade	($32.99)
Ratio avg win/avg loss	.88	Avg trade (win & loss)	$13.04
Max consec. Winners	7	Max consec. losers	2
Avg # bars in winners	2	Avg # bars in losers	2
Max intraday drawdown		($99.77)	
Profit Factor	2.53	Max # contracts held	99

TradeStation Strategy Performance Report - Lambda SUNW-Daily (1/2/90-1/31/00)

Performance Summary: All Trades

Total Net Profit	$746.96	Open position P/L	$0.00
Gross Profit	$1,480.33	Gross Loss	($733.37)
Total # of trades	47	Percent profitable	68.09%
Number winning trades	32	Number losing trades	15
Largest winning trade	$91.19	Largest losing trade	($127.04)
Average winning trade	$46.26	Average losing trade	($48.89)
Ratio avg win/avg loss	.95	Avg trade (win & loss)	$15.89
Max consec. Winners	10	Max consec. losers	3
Avg # bars in winners	3	Avg # bars in losers	2
Max intraday drawdown		($207.57)	
Profit Factor	2.02	Max # contracts held	976

TradeStation Strategy Performance Report - Lambda WMT-
Daily (1/2/90-1/31/00)

Performance Summary: All Trades

Total Net Profit	$377.78	Open position P/L	$0.00
Gross Profit	$574.85	Gross Loss	($197.07)
Total # of trades	29	Percent profitable	72.41%
Number winning trades	21	Number losing trades	8
Largest winning trade	$40.25	Largest losing trade	($28.88)
Average winning trade	$27.37	Average losing trade	($24.63)
Ratio avg win/avg loss	1.11	Avg trade (win & loss)	$13.03
Max consec. Winners	8	Max consec. losers	2
Avg # bars in winners	2	Avg # bars in losers	4
Max intraday drawdown		($58.84)	
Profit Factor	2.92	Max # contracts held	187

205

3L-R Pattern

Pattern Type: Exact

Entry Signal Type: Long

Order Entry Point: Open of tomorrow

Applicable Stocks:

Symbol	Profit Target %	Stop-loss %
C	9	9
CA	8	8
CHV	5	5
CMGI	5	5
DD	5	5
GE	7	7
GM	8	8
HD	6	6
INTC	6	6
JNJ	9	9
KO	6	6
MSFT	4	4
PG	7	7

Bar Sequence Length: 4

Bar Sequence: $S = \{(H_0), (L_1), (L_2), (L_3, H_3)\}$

Graphical Representation:

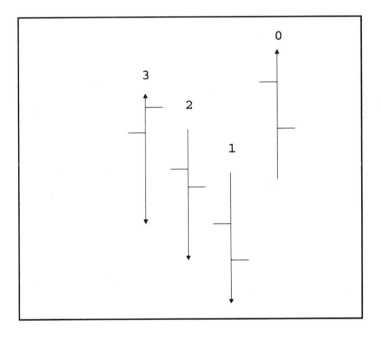

Easy Language Code

```
{****************************************************
Description  : 3L-R Pattern Entry Signal
Developed By : Michael Harris
****************************************************}

if l[1] < l[2] and l[2] < l[3] and h[0] > h[3] then
            buy  ("3L-R") next bar on the open;


{****************************************************
Description  : 3L-R Pattern Long Exit Signal
Developed By : Michael Harris
Comments: ptarget and stopl are in percentage terms
****************************************************}
variables: profitprice(0), stopprice(0);
input: ptarget(0), stopl(0);

profitprice = entryprice*(1+ptarget/100);
stopprice = entryprice*(1-stopl/100);

if marketposition =1 then begin
        exitlong ("3L-R Exit") at profitprice limit;
        exitlong ("3L-R Stop") at stopprice stop;
end;
```

TradeStation Strategy Performance Report - 3L-R C-Daily (1/3/94-1/31/00)

Performance Summary: All Trades

Total Net Profit	$1,086.28	Open position P/L	$0.00
Gross Profit	$1,718.11	Gross Loss	($631.83)
Total # of trades	25	Percent profitable	72.00%
Number winning trades	18	Number losing trades	7
Largest winning trade	$132.01	Largest losing trade	($94.02)
Average winning trade	$95.45	Average losing trade	($90.26)
Ratio avg win/avg loss	1.06	Avg trade (win & loss)	$43.45
Max consec. Winners	8	Max consec. losers	2
Avg # bars in winners	16	Avg # bars in losers	18
Max intraday drawdown		($272.54)	
Profit Factor	2.72	Max # contracts held	134

TradeStation Strategy Performance Report - 3L-R CA-Daily (1/2/90-1/31/00)

Performance Summary: All Trades

Total Net Profit	$1,384.47	Open position P/L	$0.00
Gross Profit	$3,723.37	Gross Loss	($2,338.90)
Total # of trades	64	Percent profitable	62.50%
Number winning trades	40	Number losing trades	24
Largest winning trade	$192.54	Largest losing trade	($293.52)
Average winning trade	$93.08	Average losing trade	($97.45)
Ratio avg win/avg loss	.96	Avg trade (win & loss)	$21.63
Max consec. Winners	6	Max consec. losers	3
Avg # bars in winners	11	Avg # bars in losers	9
Max intraday drawdown		($452.02)	
Profit Factor	1.59	Max # contracts held	532

TradeStation Strategy Performance Report - 3L-R CHV-Daily
(1/2/90-1/31/00)

Performance Summary: All Trades

Total Net Profit	$766.57	Open position P/L	$0.00
Gross Profit	$1,627.05	Gross Loss	($860.48)
Total # of trades	50	Percent profitable	66.00%
Number winning trades	33	Number losing trades	17
Largest winning trade	$78.75	Largest losing trade	($62.08)
Average winning trade	$49.30	Average losing trade	($50.62)
Ratio avg win/avg loss	.97	Avg trade (win & loss)	$15.33
Max consec. Winners	11	Max consec. losers	2
Avg # bars in winners	12	Avg # bars in losers	13
Max intraday drawdown		($156.93)	
Profit Factor	1.89	Max # contracts held	31

TradeStation Strategy Performance Report - 3L-R CMGI-Daily
(1/26/94-1/31/00)

Performance Summary: All Trades

Total Net Profit	$1,503.09	Open position P/L	$0.00
Gross Profit	$2,273.62	Gross Loss	($770.53)
Total # of trades	21	Percent profitable	71.43%
Number winning trades	15	Number losing trades	6
Largest winning trade	$372.33	Largest losing trade	($253.77)
Average winning trade	$151.57	Average losing trade	($128.42)
Ratio avg win/avg loss	1.18	Avg trade (win & loss)	$71.58
Max consec. Winners	3	Max consec. losers	1
Avg # bars in winners	11	Avg # bars in losers	7
Max intraday drawdown		($272.73)	
Profit Factor	2.95	Max # contracts held	4,672

TradeStation Strategy Performance Report - 3L-R DD-Daily (1/2/90-1/31/00)

Performance Summary: All Trades

Total Net Profit	$1,077.26	Open position P/L	$0.00
Gross Profit	$2,109.54	Gross Loss	($1,032.29)
Total # of trades	59	Percent profitable	66.10%
Number winning trades	39	Number losing trades	20
Largest winning trade	$127.12	Largest losing trade	($60.00)
Average winning trade	$54.09	Average losing trade	($51.61)
Ratio avg win/avg loss	1.05	Avg trade (win & loss)	$18.26
Max consec. Winners	8	Max consec. losers	3
Avg # bars in winners	9	Avg # bars in losers	14
Max intraday drawdown		($206.23)	
Profit Factor	2.04	Max # contracts held	57

TradeStation Strategy Performance Report - 3L-R GE-Daily (1/2/90-1/31/00)

Performance Summary: All Trades

Total Net Profit	$1,100.00	Open position P/L	$0.00
Gross Profit	$2,095.40	Gross Loss	($995.41)
Total # of trades	44	Percent profitable	68.18%
Number winning trades	30	Number losing trades	14
Largest winning trade	$82.50	Largest losing trade	($79.50)
Average winning trade	$69.85	Average losing trade	($71.10)
Ratio avg win/avg loss	.98	Avg trade (win & loss)	$25.00
Max consec. Winners	9	Max consec. losers	3
Avg # bars in winners	31	Avg # bars in losers	14
Max intraday drawdown		($251.15)	
Profit Factor	2.11	Max # contracts held	73

TradeStation Strategy Performance Report - 3L-R GM-Daily (1/2/90-1/31/00)

Performance Summary: All Trades

Total Net Profit	$1,170.29	Open position P/L	$0.00
Gross Profit	$2,195.30	Gross Loss	($1,025.01)
Total # of trades	39	Percent profitable	69.23%
Number winning trades	27	Number losing trades	12
Largest winning trade	$98.45	Largest losing trade	($154.26)
Average winning trade	$81.31	Average losing trade	($85.42)
Ratio avg win/avg loss	.95	Avg trade (win & loss)	$30.01
Max consec. Winners	6	Max consec. losers	3
Avg # bars in winners	19	Avg # bars in losers	31
Max intraday drawdown		($298.66)	
Profit Factor	2.14	Max # contracts held	36

TradeStation Strategy Performance Report - 3L-R HD-Daily (1/2/90-1/31/00)

Performance Summary: All Trades

Total Net Profit	$1,126.70	Open position P/L	$0.00
Gross Profit	$2,073.57	Gross Loss	($946.87)
Total # of trades	46	Percent profitable	69.57%
Number winning trades	32	Number losing trades	14
Largest winning trade	$96.79	Largest losing trade	($83.91)
Average winning trade	$64.80	Average losing trade	($67.63)
Ratio avg win/avg loss	.96	Avg trade (win & loss)	$24.49
Max consec. Winners	7	Max consec. losers	3
Avg # bars in winners	15	Avg # bars in losers	8
Max intraday drawdown		($238.09)	
Profit Factor	2.19	Max # contracts held	444

TradeStation Strategy Performance Report - 3L-R INTC-Daily
(1/2/90-1/31/00)

Performance Summary: All Trades

Total Net Profit	$1,312.33	Open position P/L	$0.00
Gross Profit	$2,849.82	Gross Loss	($1,537.49)
Total # of trades	63	Percent profitable	65.08%
Number winning trades	41	Number losing trades	22
Largest winning trade	$132.71	Largest losing trade	($123.00)
Average winning trade	$69.51	Average losing trade	($69.89)
Ratio avg win/avg loss	.99	Avg trade (win & loss)	$20.83
Max consec. Winners	6	Max consec. losers	3
Avg # bars in winners	10	Avg # bars in losers	6
Max intraday drawdown		($261.77)	
Profit Factor	1.85	Max # contracts held	488

TradeStation Strategy Performance Report - 3L-R JNJ-Daily
(1/2/90-1/31/00)

Performance Summary: All Trades

Total Net Profit	$997.73	Open position P/L	$0.00
Gross Profit	$2,262.63	Gross Loss	($1,264.90)
Total # of trades	40	Percent profitable	65.00%
Number winning trades	26	Number losing trades	14
Largest winning trade	$95.87	Largest losing trade	($93.32)
Average winning trade	$87.02	Average losing trade	($90.35)
Ratio avg win/avg loss	.96	Avg trade (win & loss)	$24.94
Max consec. Winners	7	Max consec. losers	4
Avg # bars in winners	26	Avg # bars in losers	32
Max intraday drawdown		($436.69)	
Profit Factor	1.79	Max # contracts held	69

TradeStation Strategy Performance Report - 3L-R KO-Daily
(1/2/90-1/31/00)

Performance Summary: All Trades

Total Net Profit	$1,197.09	Open position P/L	$0.00
Gross Profit	$2,131.43	Gross Loss	($934.34)
Total # of trades	49	Percent profitable	69.39%
Number winning trades	34	Number losing trades	15
Largest winning trade	$76.84	Largest losing trade	($73.13)
Average winning trade	$62.69	Average losing trade	($62.29)
Ratio avg win/avg loss	1.01	Avg trade (win & loss)	$24.43
Max consec. Winners	9	Max consec. losers	2
Avg # bars in winners	23	Avg # bars in losers	16
Max intraday drawdown		($196.27)	
Profit Factor	2.28	Max # contracts held	115

TradeStation Strategy Performance Report - 3L-R MSFT-Daily
(1/2/90-1/31/00)

Performance Summary: All Trades

Total Net Profit	$1,053.43	Open position P/L	$0.00
Gross Profit	$2,196.78	Gross Loss	($1,143.35)
Total # of trades	66	Percent profitable	65.15%
Number winning trades	43	Number losing trades	23
Largest winning trade	$102.14	Largest losing trade	($84.37)
Average winning trade	$51.09	Average losing trade	($49.71)
Ratio avg win/avg loss	1.03	Avg trade (win & loss)	$15.96
Max consec. Winners	9	Max consec. losers	3
Avg # bars in winners	7	Avg # bars in losers	7
Max intraday drawdown		($170.24)	
Profit Factor	1.92	Max # contracts held	587

TradeStation Strategy Performance Report - 3L-R PG-Daily
(1/2/90-1/31/00)

Performance Summary: All Trades

Total Net Profit	$1,044.68	Open position P/L	$0.00
Gross Profit	$1,956.54	Gross Loss	($911.86)
Total # of trades	41	Percent profitable	68.29%
Number winning trades	28	Number losing trades	13
Largest winning trade	$76.25	Largest losing trade	($75.02)
Average winning trade	$69.88	Average losing trade	($70.14)
Ratio avg win/avg loss	1.00	Avg trade (win & loss)	$25.48
Max consec. Winners	11	Max consec. losers	2
Avg # bars in winners	28	Avg # bars in losers	24
Max intraday drawdown		($153.59)	
Profit Factor	2.15	Max # contracts held	61

TradeStation Strategy Performance Report - 3L-R S-Daily
(1/2/90-1/31/00)

Performance Summary: All Trades

Total Net Profit	$1,296.09	Open position P/L	$0.00
Gross Profit	$2,431.45	Gross Loss	($1,135.36)
Total # of trades	40	Percent profitable	70.00%
Number winning trades	28	Number losing trades	12
Largest winning trade	$132.40	Largest losing trade	($134.18)
Average winning trade	$86.84	Average losing trade	($94.61)
Ratio avg win/avg loss	.92	Avg trade (win & loss)	$32.40
Max consec. Winners	9	Max consec. losers	3
Avg # bars in winners	23	Avg # bars in losers	24
Max intraday drawdown		($440.65)	
Profit Factor	2.14	Max # contracts held	103

DOWN-5C Pattern

Pattern Type: Exact

Entry Signal Type: Long

Order Entry Point: Close of today

Applicable Stocks:

Symbol	Profit Target %	Stop-loss %
AMZN	8	8
AXP	7	7
C	6	6
CAT	7	7
DD	2	2
EBAY	4	4
GE	7	7
HD	7	7
HWP	8	8
INTC	3	3
IP	6	6
JNJ	7	7
KO	8	8
MCD	8	8
MRK	5	5
MSFT	2	2
ORCL	5	5
PG	8	8
T	2	2
WMT	8	8

Bar Sequence Length: 5

Bar Sequence: $S = \{(C_0), (C_1), (C_2), (C_3), (C_4)\}$

Graphical Representation:

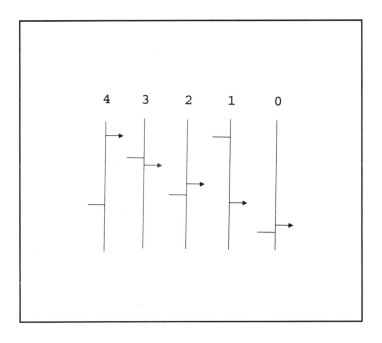

Easy language Code

```
{****************************************************
Description   : DOWN-5C Pattern Entry Signal
Developed By : Michael Harris
****************************************************}

if c[4] > c[3] and c[3] > c[2] and c[2] > c[1] and c[1] > c[0] then
        buy  ("DOWN-5C") this bar on the close;


{****************************************************
Description   : DOWN-5C Pattern Long Exit Signal
Developed By : Michael Harris
Comments: ptarget and stopl are in percentage terms
****************************************************}
variables: profitprice(0), stopprice(0);
input: ptarget(0), stopl(0);

profitprice = entryprice*(1+ptarget/100);
stopprice = entryprice*(1-stopl/100);

if marketposition =1 then begin
        exitlong ("DOWN 5-C Exit") at profitprice limit;
        exitlong ("DOWN 5-C Stop") at stopprice stop;
end;
```

TradeStation Strategy Performance Report - DOWN-5C
AMZN-Daily (5/15/97-1/31/00)

Performance Summary: All Trades

Total Net Profit	$404.62	Open position P/L	$0.00
Gross Profit	$1,218.76	Gross Loss	($814.14)
Total # of trades	20	Percent profitable	65.00%
Number winning trades	13	Number losing trades	7
Largest winning trade	$135.00	Largest losing trade	($277.70)
Average winning trade	$93.75	Average losing trade	($116.31)
Ratio avg win/avg loss	.81	Avg trade (win & loss)	$20.23
Max consec. Winners	5	Max consec. losers	2
Avg # bars in winners	3	Avg # bars in losers	3
Max intraday drawdown		($286.65)	
Profit Factor	1.50	Max # contracts held	253

TradeStation Strategy Performance Report - DOWN-5C AXP-
Daily (1/2/90-1/31/00)

Performance Summary: All Trades

Total Net Profit	$1,766.78	Open position P/L	$0.00
Gross Profit	$2,775.27	Gross Loss	($1,008.49)
Total # of trades	53	Percent profitable	73.58%
Number winning trades	39	Number losing trades	14
Largest winning trade	$121.80	Largest losing trade	($83.41)
Average winning trade	$71.16	Average losing trade	($72.03)
Ratio avg win/avg loss	.99	Avg trade (win & loss)	$33.34
Max consec. Winners	6	Max consec. losers	2
Avg # bars in winners	15	Avg # bars in losers	12
Max intraday drawdown		($152.24)	
Profit Factor	2.75	Max # contracts held	63

TradeStation Strategy Performance Report - DOWN-5C C-
Daily (1/3/94-1/31/00)

Performance Summary: All Trades

Total Net Profit	$1,584.31	Open position P/L	$0.00
Gross Profit	$2,032.55	Gross Loss	($448.24)
Total # of trades	37	Percent profitable	81.08%
Number winning trades	30	Number losing trades	7
Largest winning trade	$127.10	Largest losing trade	($77.80)
Average winning trade	$67.75	Average losing trade	($64.03)
Ratio avg win/avg loss	1.06	Avg trade (win & loss)	$42.82
Max consec. Winners	7	Max consec. losers	2
Avg # bars in winners	12	Avg # bars in losers	5
Max intraday drawdown		($160.25)	
Profit Factor	4.53	Max # contracts held	141

TradeStation Strategy Performance Report - DOWN-5C CAT-
Daily (1/2/90-1/31/00)

Performance Summary: All Trades

Total Net Profit	$2,075.89	Open position P/L	$0.00
Gross Profit	$3,615.78	Gross Loss	($1,539.89)
Total # of trades	67	Percent profitable	71.64%
Number winning trades	48	Number losing trades	19
Largest winning trade	$115.50	Largest losing trade	($130.50)
Average winning trade	$75.33	Average losing trade	($81.05)
Ratio avg win/avg loss	.93	Avg trade (win & loss)	$30.98
Max consec. Winners	9	Max consec. losers	4
Avg # bars in winners	15	Avg # bars in losers	12
Max intraday drawdown		($383.78)	
Profit Factor	2.35	Max # contracts held	100

TradeStation Strategy Performance Report - DOWN-5C DD-
Daily (1/2/90-1/31/00)

Performance Summary: All Trades

Total Net Profit	$475.15	Open position P/L	$0.00
Gross Profit	$1,085.80	Gross Loss	($610.65)
Total # of trades	69	Percent profitable	63.77%
Number winning trades	44	Number losing trades	25
Largest winning trade	$54.63	Largest losing trade	($64.80)
Average winning trade	$24.68	Average losing trade	($24.43)
Ratio avg win/avg loss	1.01	Avg trade (win & loss)	$6.89
Max consec. Winners	16	Max consec. losers	4
Avg # bars in winners	3	Avg # bars in losers	3
Max intraday drawdown		($146.05)	
Profit Factor	1.78	Max # contracts held	62

TradeStation Strategy Performance Report - DOWN-5C EBAY-
Daily (9/24/98-1/31/00)

Performance Summary: All Trades

Total Net Profit	$533.68	Open position P/L	$0.00
Gross Profit	$828.87	Gross Loss	($295.19)
Total # of trades	16	Percent profitable	75.00%
Number winning trades	12	Number losing trades	4
Largest winning trade	$206.38	Largest losing trade	($102.43)
Average winning trade	$69.07	Average losing trade	($73.80)
Ratio avg win/avg loss	.94	Avg trade (win & loss)	$33.36
Max consec. Winners	7	Max consec. losers	2
Avg # bars in winners	2	Avg # bars in losers	2
Max intraday drawdown		($153.38)	
Profit Factor	2.81	Max # contracts held	17

TradeStation Strategy Performance Report - DOWN-5C GE-Daily (1/2/90-1/31/00)

Performance Summary: All Trades

Total Net Profit	$1,225.43	Open position P/L	$0.00
Gross Profit	$2,028.14	Gross Loss	($802.71)
Total # of trades	40	Percent profitable	72.50%
Number winning trades	29	Number losing trades	11
Largest winning trade	$80.00	Largest losing trade	($85.25)
Average winning trade	$69.94	Average losing trade	($72.97)
Ratio avg win/avg loss	.96	Avg trade (win & loss)	$30.64
Max consec. Winners	10	Max consec. losers	4
Avg # bars in winners	34	Avg # bars in losers	23
Max intraday drawdown		($373.22)	
Profit Factor	2.53	Max # contracts held	74

TradeStation Strategy Performance Report - DOWN-5C HD-Daily (1/2/90-1/31/00)

Performance Summary: All Trades

Total Net Profit	$2,198.48	Open position P/L	$8.50
Gross Profit	$3,161.05	Gross Loss	($962.57)
Total # of trades	53	Percent profitable	75.47%
Number winning trades	40	Number losing trades	13
Largest winning trade	$123.48	Largest losing trade	($83.66)
Average winning trade	$79.03	Average losing trade	($74.04)
Ratio avg win/avg loss	1.07	Avg trade (win & loss)	$41.48
Max consec. Winners	9	Max consec. losers	2
Avg # bars in winners	14	Avg # bars in losers	12
Max intraday drawdown		($207.23)	
Profit Factor	3.28	Max # contracts held	561

TradeStation Strategy Performance Report - DOWN-5C HWP-Daily (1/2/90-1/31/00)

Performance Summary: All Trades

Total Net Profit	$1,669.25	Open position P/L	($4.50)
Gross Profit	$3,374.30	Gross Loss	($1,705.05)
Total # of trades	61	Percent profitable	67.21%
Number winning trades	41	Number losing trades	20
Largest winning trade	$97.32	Largest losing trade	($116.82)
Average winning trade	$82.30	Average losing trade	($85.25)
Ratio avg win/avg loss	.97	Avg trade (win & loss)	$27.36
Max consec. Winners	10	Max consec. losers	3
Avg # bars in winners	12	Avg # bars in losers	15
Max intraday drawdown		($323.11)	
Profit Factor	1.98	Max # contracts held	150

TradeStation Strategy Performance Report - DOWN-5C INTC-Daily (1/2/90-1/31/00)

Performance Summary: All Trades

Total Net Profit	$1,059.88	Open position P/L	$0.00
Gross Profit	$2,262.57	Gross Loss	($1,202.69)
Total # of trades	74	Percent profitable	63.51%
Number winning trades	47	Number losing trades	27
Largest winning trade	$111.07	Largest losing trade	($117.88)
Average winning trade	$48.14	Average losing trade	($44.54)
Ratio avg win/avg loss	1.08	Avg trade (win & loss)	$14.32
Max consec. Winners	7	Max consec. losers	3
Avg # bars in winners	4	Avg # bars in losers	3
Max intraday drawdown		($205.66)	
Profit Factor	1.88	Max # contracts held	549

TradeStation Strategy Performance Report - DOWN-5C IP-Daily (1/2/90-1/31/00)

Performance Summary: All Trades

Total Net Profit	$1,923.00	Open position P/L	($2.50)
Gross Profit	$3,025.09	Gross Loss	($1,102.09)
Total # of trades	67	Percent profitable	73.13%
Number winning trades	49	Number losing trades	18
Largest winning trade	$80.90	Largest losing trade	($76.57)
Average winning trade	$61.74	Average losing trade	($61.23)
Ratio avg win/avg loss	1.01	Avg trade (win & loss)	$28.70
Max consec. Winners	12	Max consec. losers	2
Avg # bars in winners	15	Avg # bars in losers	17
Max intraday drawdown		($175.46)	
Profit Factor	2.74	Max # contracts held	42

TradeStation Strategy Performance Report - DOWN-5C JNJ-Daily (1/2/90-1/31/00)

Performance Summary: All Trades

Total Net Profit	$1,270.11	Open position P/L	$0.00
Gross Profit	$2,481.22	Gross Loss	($1,211.11)
Total # of trades	52	Percent profitable	67.31%
Number winning trades	35	Number losing trades	17
Largest winning trade	$76.95	Largest losing trade	($82.96)
Average winning trade	$70.89	Average losing trade	($71.24)
Ratio avg win/avg loss	1.00	Avg trade (win & loss)	$24.43
Max consec. Winners	5	Max consec. losers	2
Avg # bars in winners	18	Avg # bars in losers	16
Max intraday drawdown		($215.91)	
Profit Factor	2.05	Max # contracts held	75

TradeStation Strategy Performance Report - DOWN-5C KO-
Daily (1/2/90-1/31/00)

Performance Summary: All Trades

Total Net Profit	$1,788.29	Open position P/L	$0.00
Gross Profit	$2,688.24	Gross Loss	($899.95)
Total # of trades	44	Percent profitable	75.00%
Number winning trades	33	Number losing trades	11
Largest winning trade	$92.37	Largest losing trade	($104.13)
Average winning trade	$81.46	Average losing trade	($81.81)
Ratio avg win/avg loss	1.00	Avg trade (win & loss)	$40.64
Max consec. Winners	9	Max consec. losers	4
Avg # bars in winners	30	Avg # bars in losers	16
Max intraday drawdown		($352.39)	
Profit Factor	2.99	Max # contracts held	119

TradeStation Strategy Performance Report - DOWN-5C MCD-
Daily (1/2/90-1/31/00)

Performance Summary: All Trades

Total Net Profit	$1,632.00	Open position P/L	$0.00
Gross Profit	$2,673.65	Gross Loss	($1,041.64)
Total # of trades	43	Percent profitable	72.09%
Number winning trades	31	Number losing trades	12
Largest winning trade	$116.25	Largest losing trade	($96.75)
Average winning trade	$86.25	Average losing trade	($86.80)
Ratio avg win/avg loss	.99	Avg trade (win & loss)	$37.95
Max consec. Winners	7	Max consec. losers	2
Avg # bars in winners	27	Avg # bars in losers	33
Max intraday drawdown		($245.90)	
Profit Factor	2.57	Max # contracts held	155

TradeStation Strategy Performance Report - DOWN-5C MRK-Daily (1/2/90-1/31/00)

Performance Summary: All Trades

Total Net Profit	$1,714.03	Open position P/L	$0.00
Gross Profit	$2,623.44	Gross Loss	($909.40)
Total # of trades	67	Percent profitable	74.63%
Number winning trades	50	Number losing trades	17
Largest winning trade	$64.65	Largest losing trade	($66.91)
Average winning trade	$52.47	Average losing trade	($53.49)
Ratio avg win/avg loss	.98	Avg trade (win & loss)	$25.58
Max consec. Winners	12	Max consec. losers	2
Avg # bars in winners	9	Avg # bars in losers	10
Max intraday drawdown		($186.64)	
Profit Factor	2.88	Max # contracts held	88

TradeStation Strategy Performance Report - DOWN-5C MSFT-Daily (1/2/90-1/31/00)

Performance Summary: All Trades

Total Net Profit	$1,587.31	Open position P/L	$0.00
Gross Profit	$2,231.02	Gross Loss	($643.71)
Total # of trades	80	Percent profitable	75.00%
Number winning trades	60	Number losing trades	20
Largest winning trade	$119.16	Largest losing trade	($63.46)
Average winning trade	$37.18	Average losing trade	($32.19)
Ratio avg win/avg loss	1.16	Avg trade (win & loss)	$19.84
Max consec. Winners	9	Max consec. losers	3
Avg # bars in winners	3	Avg # bars in losers	3
Max intraday drawdown		($129.57)	
Profit Factor	3.47	Max # contracts held	834

TradeStation Strategy Performance Report - DOWN-5C
ORCL-Daily (1/2/90-1/31/00)

Performance Summary: All Trades

Total Net Profit	$3,007.79	Open position P/L	$0.00
Gross Profit	$4,421.82	Gross Loss	($1,414.03)
Total # of trades	59	Percent profitable	74.58%
Number winning trades	44	Number losing trades	15
Largest winning trade	$437.64	Largest losing trade	($327.94)
Average winning trade	$100.50	Average losing trade	($94.27)
Ratio avg win/avg loss	1.07	Avg trade (win & loss)	$50.98
Max consec. Winners	8	Max consec. losers	2
Avg # bars in winners	7	Avg # bars in losers	9
Max intraday drawdown		($511.38)	
Profit Factor	3.13	Max # contracts held	3,436

TradeStation Strategy Performance Report - DOWN-5C PG-
Daily (1/2/90-1/31/00)

Performance Summary: All Trades

Total Net Profit	$2,074.43	Open position P/L	($14.63)
Gross Profit	$2,724.51	Gross Loss	($650.08)
Total # of trades	42	Percent profitable	80.95%
Number winning trades	34	Number losing trades	8
Largest winning trade	$86.67	Largest losing trade	($96.23)
Average winning trade	$80.13	Average losing trade	($81.26)
Ratio avg win/avg loss	.99	Avg trade (win & loss)	$49.39
Max consec. Winners	16	Max consec. losers	2
Avg # bars in winners	36	Avg # bars in losers	20
Max intraday drawdown		($209.26)	
Profit Factor	4.19	Max # contracts held	64

TradeStation Strategy Performance Report - DOWN-5C T-Daily (1/2/90-1/31/00)

Performance Summary: All Trades

Total Net Profit	$492.18	Open position P/L	$0.00
Gross Profit	$1,002.04	Gross Loss	($509.86)
Total # of trades	63	Percent profitable	65.08%
Number winning trades	41	Number losing trades	22
Largest winning trade	$58.58	Largest losing trade	($45.49)
Average winning trade	$24.44	Average losing trade	($23.18)
Ratio avg win/avg loss	1.05	Avg trade (win & loss)	$7.81
Max consec. Winners	6	Max consec. losers	4
Avg # bars in winners	4	Avg # bars in losers	5
Max intraday drawdown		($93.44)	
Profit Factor	1.97	Max # contracts held	63

TradeStation Strategy Performance Report - DOWN-5C WMT-Daily (1/2/90-1/31/00)

Performance Summary: All Trades

Total Net Profit	$1,663.34	Open position P/L	$0.00
Gross Profit	$2,926.91	Gross Loss	($1,263.57)
Total # of trades	50	Percent profitable	50.00%
Number winning trades	35	Number losing trades	15
Largest winning trade	$95.90	Largest losing trade	($103.36)
Average winning trade	$83.63	Average losing trade	($84.24)
Ratio avg win/avg loss	.99	Avg trade (win & loss)	$33.27
Max consec. Winners	9	Max consec. losers	3
Avg # bars in winners	20	Avg # bars in losers	19
Max intraday drawdown		($293.40)	
Profit Factor	2.32	Max # contracts held	192

OBB Pattern

Pattern Type: Exact

Entry Signal Type: Long

Order Entry Point: Close of today

Applicable Stocks:

Symbol	Profit Target %	Stop-loss %
AXP	7	7
CHV	7	7
HD	5	5
HWP	4	4
INTC	7	7
IBM	4	4
JNJ	5	5
KO	6	6
MSFT	8	8
PG	7	7
WMT	8	8

Bar Sequence Length: 3

Bar Sequence: $S = \{(H_0, L_0), (H_1, L_1), (H_2, L_2)\}$

Graphical Representation:

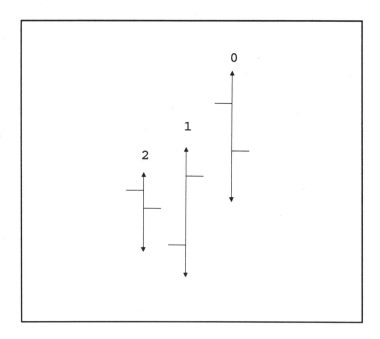

Easy Language Code

```
{*****************************************************
Description   : OBB Pattern Entry Signal
Developed By : Michael Harris
****************************************************}

if h[0] > h[1] and h[1] > h[2] and h[2] > l[0] and l[0] > l[2] and
l[2] > l[1] then
             buy  ("OBB") this bar on the close;


{*****************************************************
Description   : OBB Pattern Long Exit Signal
Developed By : Michael Harris
Comments: ptarget and stopl are in percentage terms
****************************************************}
variables: profitprice(0), stopprice(0);
input: ptarget(0), stopl(0);

profitprice = entryprice*(1+ptarget/100);
stopprice = entryprice*(1-stopl/100);

if marketposition =1 then begin
        exitlong ("OBB Exit") at profitprice limit;
        exitlong ("OBB Stop") at stopprice stop;
end;
```

TradeStation Strategy Performance Report - OBB AXP-Daily
(1/2/90-1/31/00)

Performance Summary: All Trades

Total Net Profit	$491.62	Open position P/L	$38.25
Gross Profit	$1,123.90	Gross Loss	($632.28)
Total # of trades	25	Percent profitable	64.00%
Number winning trades	16	Number losing trades	9
Largest winning trade	$76.22	Largest losing trade	($73.42)
Average winning trade	$70.24	Average losing trade	($70.25)
Ratio avg win/avg loss	1.00	Avg trade (win & loss)	$19.66
Max consec. Winners	4	Max consec. losers	2
Avg # bars in winners	16	Avg # bars in losers	18
Max intraday drawdown		($207.67)	
Profit Factor	1.78	Max # contracts held	58

TradeStation Strategy Performance Report - OBB CHV-Daily
(1/2/90-1/31/00)

Performance Summary: All Trades

Total Net Profit	$567.24	Open position P/L	$0.00
Gross Profit	$1,121.05	Gross Loss	($553.81)
Total # of trades	24	Percent profitable	66.67%
Number winning trades	16	Number losing trades	8
Largest winning trade	$72.53	Largest losing trade	($71.88)
Average winning trade	$70.07	Average losing trade	($69.23)
Ratio avg win/avg loss	1.01	Avg trade (win & loss)	$23.63
Max consec. Winners	4	Max consec. losers	2
Avg # bars in winners	31	Avg # bars in losers	46
Max intraday drawdown		($142.01)	
Profit Factor	2.02	Max # contracts held	32

TradeStation Strategy Performance Report - OBB HD-Daily
(1/2/90-1/31/00)

Performance Summary: All Trades

Total Net Profit	$683.24	Open position P/L	$0.00
Gross Profit	$1,131.44	Gross Loss	($448.20)
Total # of trades	27	Percent profitable	70.37%
Number winning trades	19	Number losing trades	8
Largest winning trade	$97.24	Largest losing trade	($62.62)
Average winning trade	$59.55	Average losing trade	($56.03)
Ratio avg win/avg loss	1.06	Avg trade (win & loss)	$25.31
Max consec. Winners	6	Max consec. losers	4
Avg # bars in winners	9	Avg # bars in losers	8
Max intraday drawdown		($254.96)	
Profit Factor	2.52	Max # contracts held	438

TradeStation Strategy Performance Report - OBB HWP-Daily
(1/2/90-1/31/00)

Performance Summary: All Trades

Total Net Profit	$423.53	Open position P/L	$0.00
Gross Profit	$1,085.19	Gross Loss	($661.66)
Total # of trades	37	Percent profitable	64.86%
Number winning trades	24	Number losing trades	13
Largest winning trade	$81.07	Largest losing trade	($81.25)
Average winning trade	$45.22	Average losing trade	($50.90)
Ratio avg win/avg loss	.89	Avg trade (win & loss)	$11.45
Max consec. Winners	5	Max consec. losers	3
Avg # bars in winners	5	Avg # bars in losers	5
Max intraday drawdown		($179.85)	
Profit Factor	1.64	Max # contracts held	119

TradeStation Strategy Performance Report - OBB IBM-Daily
(1/2/90-1/31/00)

Performance Summary: All Trades

Total Net Profit	$723.74	Open position P/L	$0.00
Gross Profit	$1,008.54	Gross Loss	($284.80)
Total # of trades 31		Percent profitable	77.42%
Number winning trades 24		Number losing trades	7
Largest winning trade	$60.90	Largest losing trade	($42.64)
Average winning trade	$42.02	Average losing trade	($40.69)
Ratio avg win/avg loss	1.03	Avg trade (win & loss)	$23.35
Max consec. Winners	5	Max consec. losers	1
Avg # bars in winners	6	Avg # bars in losers	5
Max intraday drawdown		($75.01)	
Profit Factor	3.54	Max # contracts held	75

TradeStation Strategy Performance Report - OBB INTC-Daily
(1/2/90-1/31/00)

Performance Summary: All Trades

Total Net Profit	$942.85	Open position P/L	$0.00
Gross Profit	$1,755.80	Gross Loss	($812.95)
Total # of trades	32	Percent profitable	68.75%
Number winning trades	22	Number losing trades	10
Largest winning trade	$115.06	Largest losing trade	($105.49)
Average winning trade	$79.81	Average losing trade	($81.30)
Ratio avg win/avg loss	.98	Avg trade (win & loss)	$29.46
Max consec. Winners	6	Max consec. losers	3
Avg # bars in winners	17	Avg # bars in losers	8
Max intraday drawdown		($336.97)	
Profit Factor	2.16	Max # contracts held	488

TradeStation Strategy Performance Report - OBB JNJ-Daily
(1/2/90-1/31/00)

Performance Summary: All Trades

Total Net Profit	$554.67	Open position P/L	$0.00
Gross Profit	$1,031.09	Gross Loss	($476.43)
Total # of trades	29	Percent profitable	68.97%
Number winning trades	20	Number losing trades	9
Largest winning trade	$55.50	Largest losing trade	($66.00)
Average winning trade	$51.55	Average losing trade	($52.94)
Ratio avg win/avg loss	.97	Avg trade (win & loss)	$19.13
Max consec. Winners	8	Max consec. losers	3
Avg # bars in winners	12	Avg # bars in losers	12
Max intraday drawdown		($157.26)	
Profit Factor	2.16	Max # contracts held	74

TradeStation Strategy Performance Report - OBB KO-Daily
(1/2/90-1/31/00)

Performance Summary: All Trades

Total Net Profit	$1,040.49	Open position P/L	$0.00
Gross Profit	$1,525.45	Gross Loss	($484.96)
Total # of trades	32	Percent profitable	75.00%
Number winning trades	24	Number losing trades	8
Largest winning trade	$75.62	Largest losing trade	($64.67)
Average winning trade	$63.56	Average losing trade	($60.62)
Ratio avg win/avg loss	1.05	Avg trade (win & loss)	$32.52
Max consec. Winners	12	Max consec. losers	3
Avg # bars in winners	25	Avg # bars in losers	10
Max intraday drawdown		($184.64)	
Profit Factor	3.15	Max # contracts held	115

TradeStation Strategy Performance Report - OBB MSFT-Daily
(1/2/90-1/31/00)

Performance Summary: All Trades

Total Net Profit	$860.98	Open position P/L	$0.00
Gross Profit	$1,942.97	Gross Loss	($1,081.98)
Total # of trades	34	Percent profitable	64.71%
Number winning trades	22	Number losing trades	12
Largest winning trade	$125.50	Largest losing trade	($117.94)
Average winning trade	$88.32	Average losing trade	($90.17)
Ratio avg win/avg loss	.98	Avg trade (win & loss)	$25.32
Max consec. Winners	5	Max consec. losers	2
Avg # bars in winners	18	Avg # bars in losers	15
Max intraday drawdown		($272.62)	
Profit Factor	1.80	Max # contracts held	674

TradeStation Strategy Performance Report - OBB PG-Daily
(1/2/90-1/31/00)

Performance Summary: All Trades

Total Net Profit	$846.93	Open position P/L	$0.00
Gross Profit	$1,486.81	Gross Loss	($639.88)
Total # of trades	30	Percent profitable	70.00%
Number winning trades	21	Number losing trades	9
Largest winning trade	$78.73	Largest losing trade	($75.02)
Average winning trade	$70.80	Average losing trade	($71.10)
Ratio avg win/avg loss	1.00	Avg trade (win & loss)	$28.23
Max consec. Winners	8	Max consec. losers	2
Avg # bars in winners	30	Avg # bars in losers	19
Max intraday drawdown		($151.95)	
Profit Factor	2.32	Max # contracts held	61

TradeStation Strategy Performance Report - OBB WMT-Daily (1/2/90-1/31/00)

Performance Summary: All Trades

Total Net Profit	$1,128.84	Open position P/L	$0.00
Gross Profit	$1,251.60	Gross Loss	($122.76)
Total # of trades	21	Percent profitable	90.48%
Number winning trades	19	Number losing trades	2
Largest winning trade	$98.46	Largest losing trade	($61.50)
Average winning trade	$65.87	Average losing trade	($61.38)
Ratio avg win/avg loss	1.07	Avg trade (win & loss)	$53.75
Max consec. Winners	11	Max consec. losers	1
Avg # bars in winners	12	Avg # bars in losers	15
Max intraday drawdown		($92.63)	
Profit Factor	10.20	Max # contracts held	176

GAP-2H Pattern

Pattern Type: Exact

Entry Signal Type: Long

Order Entry Point: Close of today

Applicable Stocks:

Symbol	Profit Target %	Stop-loss %
GE	7	7
HD	7	7
INTC	8	8
MRK	7	7
ORCL	8	8
WMT	8	8
JNJ	8	8

Bar Sequence Length: 3

Bar Sequence: $S = \{(H_0, L_0), (H_1, L_1), (H_2, L_2)\}$

Graphical Representation:

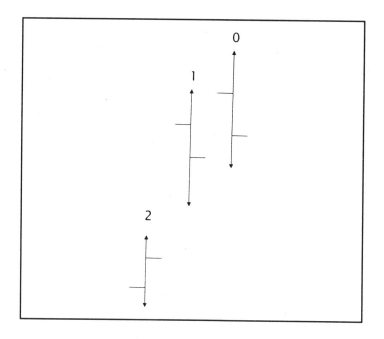

Easy Language Code

```
{***********************************************

Description   : GAP-2H Pattern Entry Signal
Developed By : Michael Harris
***********************************************}
if h[0] > h[1] and h[1] > l[0] and l[0] > l[1] and l[1] > h[2]
and
        h[2] > l[2] then
                buy  ("GPA-2H") this bar on the close;


{***********************************************

Description   : GAP-2H Pattern Long Exit Signal
Developed By : Michael Harris
Comments: ptarget and stopl are in percentage terms
***********************************************}
variables: profitprice(0), stopprice(0);
input: ptarget(0), stopl(0);

profitprice = entryprice*(1+ptarget/100);
stopprice = entryprice*(1-stopl/100);

if marketposition =1 then begin
        exitlong ("GAP-2H Exit") at profitprice limit;
        exitlong ("GAP-2H Stop") at stopprice stop;
end;
```

TradeStation Strategy Performance Report - GAP-2H GE-Daily (1/2/90-1/31/00)

Performance Summary: All Trades

Total Net Profit	$916.83	Open position P/L	$0.00
Gross Profit	$1,336.10	Gross Loss	($419.27)
Total # of trades	25	Percent profitable	76.00%
Number winning trades	19	Number losing trades	6
Largest winning trade	$76.10	Largest losing trade	($74.57)
Average winning trade	$70.32	Average losing trade	($69.88)
Ratio avg win/avg loss	1.01	Avg trade (win & loss)	$36.67
Max consec. Winners	6	Max consec. losers	2
Avg # bars in winners	35	Avg # bars in losers	36
Max intraday drawdown		($148.25)	
Profit Factor	3.19	Max # contracts held	72

TradeStation Strategy Performance Report - GAP-2H HD-Daily (1/2/90-1/31/00)

Performance Summary: All Trades

Total Net Profit	$1,373.48	Open position P/L	$0.00
Gross Profit	$2,332.89	Gross Loss	($959.41)
Total # of trades	43	Percent profitable	72.09%
Number winning trades	31	Number losing trades	12
Largest winning trade	$102.40	Largest losing trade	($96.43)
Average winning trade	$75.25	Average losing trade	($79.95)
Ratio avg win/avg loss	.94	Avg trade (win & loss)	$31.94
Max consec. Winners	6	Max consec. losers	4
Avg # bars in winners	21	Avg # bars in losers	19
Max intraday drawdown		($409.88)	
Profit Factor	2.43	Max # contracts held	535

TradeStation Strategy Performance Report - GAP-2H INTC-Daily (1/2/90-1/31/00)

Performance Summary: All Trades

Total Net Profit	$1,850.61	Open position P/L	$0.00
Gross Profit	$2,659.74	Gross Loss	($809.14)
Total # of trades	40	Percent profitable	77.50%
Number winning trades	31	Number losing trades	9
Largest winning trade	$111.83	Largest losing trade	($121.35)
Average winning trade	$85.80	Average losing trade	($89.90)
Ratio avg win/avg loss	.95	Avg trade (win & loss)	$46.27
Max consec. Winners	7	Max consec. losers	2
Avg # bars in winners	14	Avg # bars in losers	19
Max intraday drawdown		($158.91)	
Profit Factor	3.29	Max # contracts held	381

TradeStation Strategy Performance Report - GAP-2H JNJ-Daily (1/2/90-1/31/00)

Performance Summary: All Trades

Total Net Profit	$878.91	Open position P/L	$0.00
Gross Profit	$1,603.66	Gross Loss	($724.75)
Total # of trades	29	Percent profitable	68.97%
Number winning trades	20	Number losing trades	9
Largest winning trade	$85.50	Largest losing trade	($91.01)
Average winning trade	$80.18	Average losing trade	($80.53)
Ratio avg win/avg loss	1.00	Avg trade (win & loss)	$30.31
Max consec. Winners	8	Max consec. losers	2
Avg # bars in winners	39	Avg # bars in losers	32
Max intraday drawdown		($239.51)	
Profit Factor	2.21	Max # contracts held	73

TradeStation Strategy Performance Report - GAP-2H MRK-Daily (1/2/90-1/31/00)

Performance Summary: All Trades

Total Net Profit	$946.36	Open position P/L	$0.00
Gross Profit	$1,580.42	Gross Loss	($634.06)
Total # of trades	31	Percent profitable	70.97%
Number winning trades	22	Number losing trades	9
Largest winning trade	$79.72	Largest losing trade	($73.87)
Average winning trade	$71.84	Average losing trade	($70.45)
Ratio avg win/avg loss	1.02	Avg trade (win & loss)	$30.53
Max consec. Winners	8	Max consec. losers	3
Avg # bars in winners	26	Avg # bars in losers	12
Max intraday drawdown		($253.11)	
Profit Factor	2.49	Max # contracts held	84

TradeStation Strategy Performance Report - GAP-2H ORCL-Daily (1/2/90-1/31/00)

Performance Summary: All Trades

Total Net Profit	$1,804.75	Open position P/L	$0.00
Gross Profit	$2,422.65	Gross Loss	($617.89)
Total # of trades	27	Percent profitable	74.07%
Number winning trades	20	Number losing trades	7
Largest winning trade	$312.90	Largest losing trade	($109.30)
Average winning trade	$121.13	Average losing trade	($88.27)
Ratio avg win/avg loss	1.37	Avg trade (win & loss)	$66.84
Max consec. Winners	9	Max consec. losers	3
Avg # bars in winners	19	Avg # bars in losers	6
Max intraday drawdown		($328.38)	
Profit Factor	3.92	Max # contracts held	2,469

TradeStation Strategy Performance Report - GAP-2H WMT-
Daily (1/2/90-1/31/00)

Performance Summary: All Trades

Total Net Profit	$970.33	Open position P/L	$0.00
Gross Profit	$1,535.12	Gross Loss	($564.78)
Total # of trades	25	Percent profitable	72.00%
Number winning trades	18	Number losing trades	7
Largest winning trade	$111.25	Largest losing trade	($85.63)
Average winning trade	$85.28	Average losing trade	($80.68)
Ratio avg win/avg loss	1.06	Avg trade (win & loss)	$38.81
Max consec. Winners	5	Max consec. losers	3
Avg # bars in winners	24	Avg # bars in losers	10
Max intraday drawdown		($310.82)	
Profit Factor	2.72	Max # contracts held	181

Reader Service Information

More information can be obtained as follows:

By Fax: (212) 898-1156

By e-mail: mkharris@hotmail.com

Web Site: www.tradingpatterns.com

By mail: Please write to:
                   Mike Harris
                   Bridge Plaza Office Center
                   29-28 41st Avenue, Suite 910B
                   LI City, NY 11101

Please include your name and your e-mail, telephone or fax number.

Index